# The Struggle
# Against Slavery
*A History in Documents*

State linked to State—Oh, Unity divine!
Our cherished Washington! the praise be thine.
And yet, alas! by thee, regarded not,
One curse remains—a monstrous, hideous blot.

But should thy spirit in new form burst forth,
The stain to 'rase that tarnishes the South;
This proffered Quilt would proudly claim to be
Spread o'er the cradle of his infancy.

# The Struggle
# Against Slavery
## *A History in Documents*

*David Waldstreicher*

# OXFORD
### UNIVERSITY PRESS

To Shane White—fellow traveler and honorary New Yorker

**General Editors**

Sarah Deutsch
*Associate Professor of History*
*University of Arizona*

Carol Karlsen
*Professor of History*
*University of Michigan*

Robert G. Moeller
*Professor of History*
*University of California, Irvine*

Jeffrey N. Wasserstrom
*Associate Professor of History*
*Indiana University*

## OXFORD
UNIVERSITY PRESS

Oxford New York

Athens  Auckland  Bangkok  Bogatá  Buenos Aires  Cape Town
Chennai Dar es Salaam  Delhi  Florence  Hong Kong  Istambul  Karachi
Kolkata  Kuala Lumpur Madrid Melbourne Mexico City  Mumbai Nairobi
Paris  São Paulo  Shanghai  Singapore  Taipei  Tokyo  Toronto  Warsaw
with associated companies in Berlin Ibadan

Copyright © 2001 by David Waldstreicher

Design: Sandy Kaufman
Layout: Loraine Machlin
Picture Research: Lisa Barnett

Published by Oxford University Press, Inc.
198 Madison Avenue, New York, New York 10016
www.oup.com

Library of Congress Cataloging-in-Publication Data
Waldstreicher, David.
The struggle against slavery : a history in documents / David Waldstreicher.
p. cm  —  (Pages from history)
Includes bibliographical references and index.
ISBN 0-19-510850-7
1. Slave insurrections—United States—History—Sources—Juvenile
literature. 2. Slaves—United States—Social conditions—Sources—
Juvenile literature. 3. Free African Americans—Social conditions—
Sources—Juvenile literature. 4. African Americans—Civil rights—
History—Sources—Juvenile literature. 5. Antislavery movements—
United States—History—Sources—Juvenile literature. I. Title. II. Series.
E447. W35 2001
306.3'62'0973—dc21
2001032941

987654321

Printed in the United States of America on acid-free paper

**Board of Advisors**

Steven Goldberg
*Social Studies Supervisor*
*New Rochelle, N.Y., Public Schools*

John Pyne
*Social Studies Supervisor*
*West Milford, N.J., Public Schools*

Cover: *Harriet Tubman, on left, was photo-*
*graphed with a group of the former slaves she led to*
*freedom. Text: From a North Carolina General*
*Assembly bill to prevent slaves from being taught*
*to read or write, 1830.*

Frontispiece: *Abolition quilt from about 1853.*

Title page: *Jack and Abby Landlord, a slave*
*couple, who at the time of this photograph from the*
*1860s were 110 and 100 years old respectively.*

# Contents

# What Is a Document?

To the historian, a document is, quite simply, any sort of historical evidence. It is a primary source, the raw material of history. A document may be more than the expected government paperwork, such as a treaty or passport. It is also a letter, diary, will, grocery list, newspaper article, recipe, memoir, oral history, school yearbook, map, chart, architectural plan, poster, musical score, play script, novel, political cartoon, painting, photograph—even an object.

Using primary sources allows us not just to read *about* history, but to read history itself. It allows us to immerse ourselves in the look and feel of an era gone by, to understand its people and their language, whether verbal or visual. And it allows us to take an active, hands-on role in (re)constructing history.

Using primary sources requires us to use our powers of detection to ferret out the relevant facts and to draw conclusions from them; just as Agatha Christie uses the scores in a bridge game to determine the identity of a murderer, the historian uses facts from a variety of sources—some, perhaps, seemingly inconsequential—to build a historical case.

The poet W. H. Auden wrote that history was the study of questions. Primary sources force us to ask questions—and then, by answering them, to construct a narrative or an argument that makes sense to us. Moreover, as we draw on the many sources from "the dust-bin of history," we can endow that narrative with character, personality, and texture—all the elements that make history so endlessly intriguing.

**Cartoon**
*This political cartoon addresses the issue of church and state. It illustrates the Supreme Court's role in balancing the demands of the First Amendment of the Constitution and the desires of the religious population.*

**Illustration**
*Illustrations from children's books, such as this alphabet from the* New England Primer, *tell us how children were educated, and also what the religious and moral values of the time were.*

A  In *Adam's* Fall
We Sinned all.

B  Thy Life to Mend
This *Book* Attend.

C  The *Cat* doth play
And after flay.

D  A *Dog* will bite
A Thief at night.

E  An *Eagles* flight
Is out of fight.

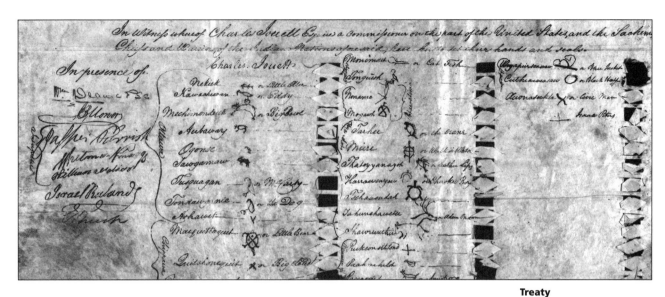

**Treaty**

*A government document such as this 1805 treaty can reveal not only the details of government policy, but information about the people who signed it. Here, the Indians' names were written in English transliteration by U.S. officials; the Indians added pictographs to the right of their names.*

**Map**

*A 1788 British map of India shows the region prior to British colonization, an indication of the kingdoms and provinces whose ethnic divisions would resurface later in India's history.*

**Literature**

*The first written version of the Old English epic Beowulf, from the late 10th century, is physical evidence of the transition from oral to written history. Charred by fire, it is also a physical record of the wear and tear of history.*

# How to Read a Document

Documents are bits of the past that have survived. They come in many shapes and sizes: texts (such as books, newspapers, magazines, and letters), pictures (such as paintings, photographs, and prints), and things (such as furniture, statues, and buildings). When we approach a document for clues into the larger past, we ask questions about what such a source can and cannot say. We ask: What does this document tell us? What were its creators trying to say or accomplish? What does it *not* tell us?

How we read a document, what we take from it, in other words, will depend on the questions we ask. Advertisements for runaway slaves, for example, were written and published in order to recapture fugitives, but they also tell us, if we care to look, many interesting things about the slaves' skills, where they had been born and lived, and how they rebelled against the system. They do not tell us, however, why the slaves ran away or what happened to them after they became fugitives.

When antislavery became a large-scale political movement in the 19th century, white and black abolitionists began to use all kinds of evidence about slaves and their lives to argue against slavery. Some of the documents in this book, such as the narratives of former slaves Olaudah Equiano, Frederick Douglass, and Harriet Jacobs, are examples of the abolitionists' efforts to document the evils of slavery and the fact of slave resistance. As documents, they tell us about slavery, but they also tell us about the nature of the fight against slavery.

**Authorship**
Especially with controversial subjects such as slavery, it is important to consider who authored the document and for what purpose. John Allwood told readers of a Charleston, South Carolina, newspaper about the skills of his slaves because he wanted to make more money when he sold them. In other documents, slave owners might downplay their slaves' abilities, because it was in the owners' interest to do so.

**Detail**
In his advertisement, Allwood asks people who owe him money to pay him before he leaves town so that he can pay his own debts. He also describes some pictures he has for sale. But these are only afterthoughts to the descriptions of the slaves for sale. This could imply that the slaves were worth more money than the debts or the goods he had to sell.

**Story**
These abolitionist trading cards, from a series of 12, tell the story of a slave who is sold, separated from his family, and whipped. He then runs away and joins the Union army during the Civil War. These cards were created to celebrate black soldiers' war efforts. The abolitionists wanted to encourage black service in the war and to transform what was a war against southern secession into a fight against slavery.

**Symbols**
In their portrayal of slavery, abolitionists often focused on the scene in which slave families were separated by the sale of one family member. Breaking the hearts of his wife and child is as bad as or worse than breaking the body of the slave. With such images, abolitionists made the point that slavery was not for the good of the slaves, as southerners maintained, and that slaves had families just as whites did.

**Pose**
How people stand, or sit, the look on their faces, and the clothes they wear are markers of status and identity. In "The Sale," the slave is depicted as dejected, looking down with his hat in hand. In "Make Way for Liberty!" the slave, now a uniformed soldier, charges forward with a determined expression. Abolitionists wanted to convey that the humility of the slave was a product of circumstances, not race.

The SUBSCRIBER,
Intending to leave the Province in APRIL next,
*WILL DISPOSE OF*
His NEGRO FELLOWS, *Painters,*
On WEDNESDAY *the* Seventh *of April* next,
*At his Yard in* Queen-Street, *directly opposite Mr.* CANNON's.

AS to their Abilities, he thinks them evident, they having transacted the Whole of his Business, without any hired Affistance; and he has taken no little Pains in initiating them in the true Principles of their Profeffion.

*L I K E W I S E,*
A good HOUSE-WENCH,
Who can wash and iron exceeding well, and is a tolerable Cook.

He has also a few well-painted Pictures to difpofe of; fome good Prints, framed and glazed; with a little Houfhold-Furniture.—The Conditions will be made known on the Day of Sale.

\*\*\* He begs thofe to whom he is indebted to fend in their Accompts for Payment;—and requefts the Favour of thofe who are indebted to him, to difcharge their Accompts; by which Means he hopes to give his Creditors general Satisfaction.

J O H N   A L L W O O D.

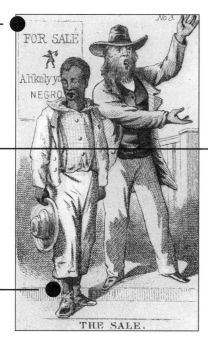

THE SALE.

THE PARTING "Buy us too."

" MAKE WAY FOR LIBERTY.!"

*Introduction*

# Vanguards of Freedom

I n colonial America slavery was not the exception—it was the rule. In the new United States of America, from the end of the American Revolution until the Civil War (1783–1861), slavery was a way of life in the southern half of the country and for the majority of African Americans who lived in the South.

And yet slavery did end. It disappeared gradually in the North and rather suddenly in the South. It ended because of wars, revolutions, and other changes that upset a system in which most Africans and their descendants were forced to work and live under the dictates of those who owned them. But slavery ended primarily because slaves, former slaves, and those whites who did not believe it was right to own other people fought against it.

This history in documents explores the various ways people, primarily those of African and mixed descent, struggled to end slavery. How could slaves and their allies fight a system designed to keep them obedient, to prevent them from speaking up or acting on their own behalf? The story is a heroic one precisely because of the obstacles faced by those who wanted to free African Americans from slavery. The institution of slavery changed over time in response to the possibility of slaves' everyday resistance, escape, and outright rebellion. Understanding how slaves themselves could fight slavery means looking for and evaluating the cracks in the economic and social system— the rules that slaves could bend for their own purposes.

A consistent pattern emerges in the history of American slavery, a pattern running through the experiences and actions of slave owners and the experiences and actions of those they held in bondage. The more work that masters expected from slaves, and the more they kept slaves in their houses and workplaces and sought to make them like children who would ideally always do what they were told, the more these masters actually gave those slaves chances to find some freedom within the system and opportunities to use their knowledge in order to escape. The more masters used their slaves to travel for them or with them, to sell their goods or to send messages, the more they enabled slaves to become knowledgeable of the path to freedom that many Europeans in America had taken: the path of moving from one place to another.

There were three kinds of heroes in the struggle against slavery: antislavery activists, rebels, and runaways. The best known of these heroes are the antislavery activists of the later period (1830–65)—people such as former slaves Frederick Douglass and Sojourner Truth who devoted their lives, or a good part of their lives, to speaking out against slavery. These antislavery activists, who believed slavery was a moral evil and a terrible national sin that should be abolished immediately, organized the abolitionist movement. By the 19th century, abolitionists were putting tremendous pressure on the slave system in those states that had not already put into law some scheme for gradually freeing slaves or their children.

Even in the northern states where slavery had been eradicated by law, most people were not abolitionists. Such was the power of the slaveholders, who threatened civil war if national laws were passed against the slave system. Only in a few places did antislavery sentiments represent a majority of white public opinion. But the dedication of these activists ensured that by the 1850s, Americans—including slaves—knew that there were alternatives. The sectional controversy between North and South had become heated during the 1830s over the question of what to do about abolitionism. Should Congress receive abolitionist petitions? Should abolitionists be allowed to circulate their literature through the mails? Southern slaveholders, by this time, depicted abolitionists as dangerous radicals bent on upsetting society. They

*This pleading slave and the slogan were the symbols of the abolitionist movement. Black and white abolitionists worked together to prove to the American public that African Americans were indeed men, and women, and to advocate for the end to slavery, which denied the slaves their fundamental human rights.*

developed a theory of racial inferiority to explain why slavery was natural, even though it had become unusual in most of the world by 1834, when slavery was abolished in the British West Indies.

Abolitionists, in turn, saw themselves as the vanguard of freedom, extending the rights and privileges granted by God or won during the American Revolution to the next group that so conspicuously lacked them: people with darker skin. (Some of the early abolitionists, such as Douglass, Truth, William Lloyd Garrison, and the Grimké sisters of South Carolina, also supported women's rights.) This later history of the antislavery movement is a story of cooperation between whites and blacks. In many ways it is a great, untold story of American history, for it shows how much a small group of people dedicated to change can accomplish, even if they themselves do not always agree on everything.

The second group of figures in the antislavery struggle, rarer and even more controversial, consisted of the slave rebels who started or participated in organized revolts. Slave rebellions occurred with enough regularity in North America to force the colonies, and later the southern states, to change the laws of slavery in order to make it very difficult for the enslaved to work together against the masters. Given the dispersed, agricultural nature of American societies, it is remarkable that slave rebellions occurred as often as they did and shaped the overall struggle against slavery so consistently. In the 19th century, antislavery activists took different stands on the question of violence. Whites tended to fear the results of slave rebellions, whereas blacks, among themselves, generally celebrated the courage and example of rebels such as Gabriel Prosser and Nat Turner, despite the failure of these men to free slaves. As more and more areas of the United States became free, or contained significant free black populations, former slaves became targets of suspicion, especially after some of them helped slaves escape or rebel.

One more group, perhaps the most important of all, linked the rebel slaves and the abolitionists: these were the fugitive, or runaway, slaves. Some scholars have noticed that in North America there were fewer slave rebellions than in the Caribbean, which had a higher proportion of slaves. Because North America was a huge territory, where plantations and towns were spread out, running away was often a better option. By the 18th century, running away became both a way for a few men and women to escape slavery and a (risky) way of negotiating with masters. Most slaves never dared to turn fugitive, but enough did to force masters, in general, to develop new ways of keeping individuals from leaving. Slaveholders began to place newspaper advertisements (with rewards) for runaways, for example, and later they organized white patrols in the South.

Individual runaways may not have been a great threat to the overall slave system, but together, and over time, they made a decisive difference. They did so in two ways. First, during the American Revolution, so many slaves ran away or negotiated their freedom that the entire history of slavery in the United States turned out to be profoundly different from the history of slavery in the American colonies. In the United States a substantial number of free blacks congregated in cities in the newly free or soon-to-be-free northern states. They provided a visible alternative to slavery that worried white southerners; more important, they formed the original and most consistent base of support for the abolitionist movement.

Runaways again changed the politics of slavery and abolition during the Civil War, a conflict itself catalyzed by the debate over slavery and its extension into new western territories. During the Civil War (1861–65), runaways upset the system of production in the war-torn South. Moreover, southern fugitives and the freeborn descendants of fugitives fought in the Union army against the South. The series of developments that ended American slavery—first, the American Revolution and then the Civil War—could not have occurred without the actions of runaway slaves and the controversies they inspired.

The most memorable and effective antislavery activists were those who had successfully escaped slavery. Figures such as Frederick Douglass (and his northern-born sons who fought in the Civil War) lived and worked at the crossroads where American history and African-American history became the same set of struggles, the same controversies. That is why this book focuses on African Americans who fought slavery. They secured freedom for themselves and their descendants, and they made American history.

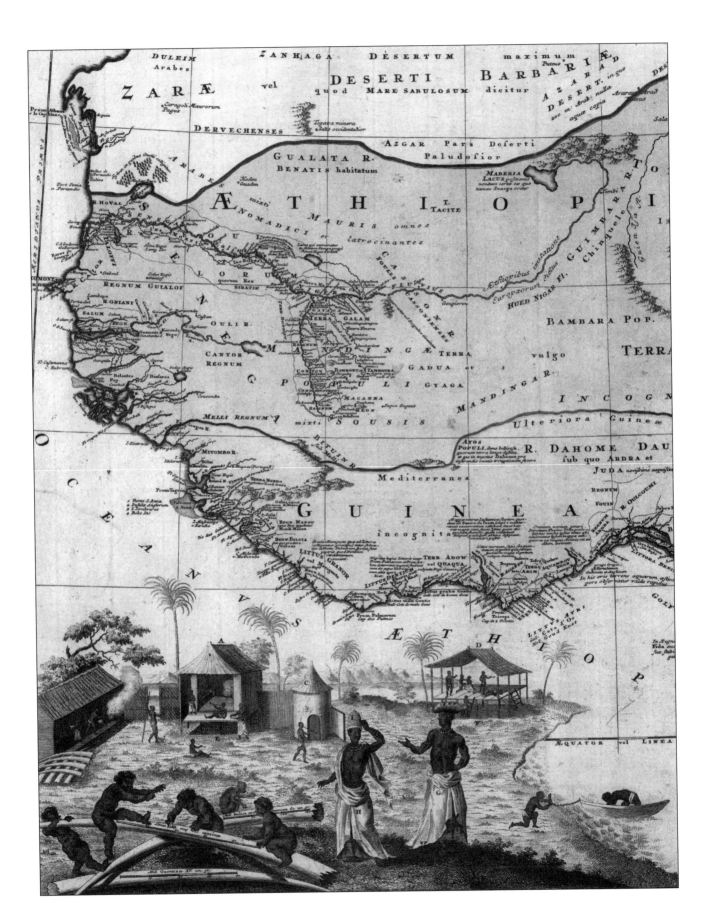

*Chapter One*

# The Making of American Slavery

S lavery did not begin in America: it had existed since ancient times all over the world, including Africa. But slavery became a special New World phenomenon in the 17th and 18th centuries. The scale of the African slave trade soon dwarfed all other ways of bringing people to the Americas. Most of these Africans were taken not to those areas that later became the United States but to Brazil and the Caribbean—where the majority died quickly under horrific working conditions. The owners of plantations in the West Indies and South America found it cheaper to import replacement slaves than to keep the ones they had alive.

Mainland North America turned out to be different in the long run. Because its tobacco and grain crops were not as spectacularly profitable as West Indian sugar, North American colonists could not afford to pay as much for laborers. Masters had to keep their slaves and indentured servants (whites, primarily, who had signed a contract to work for a certain number of years) in better health. African slaves arrived on the mainland only 12 years after the settlement at Jamestown in 1607. Many of the first slaves in the New World were people from the West African coastal areas. Often they knew more languages, and had more experience in world trade, than their masters. A few of them managed to work their way to freedom, acquiring their own farms in Virginia by the 1660s and 1670s.

Wherever agriculture or other forms of producing goods for the international market became highly profitable in North America—in Virginia during the 1680s, Pennsylvania and New York in the early 1700s, South Carolina throughout its early history—the slave population grew. In Virginia during the early period and throughout the 17th and 18th centuries to the north, slavery coexisted with other systems

*This mid-18th-century map of the West African coast shows the main ports of the slave trade, and is illustrated with a scene depicting the main European export from this part of the world—Africans.*

*An African American boy serves tea to a Rhode Island family in this painting from around 1740. Northern slaves and free blacks often worked as household servants and at various crafts, rather than in the fields like many southern slaves.*

of labor, such as the use of imported indentured servants. Even in the relatively cold northern states, where slaves did not work the fields, slavery became important to the economy in the 18th century. Africans and their descendants did every kind of job, from sailing ships to waiting at tables to dressing the wigs that had become fashionable among the upper classes. They became the muscle, and in many ways the joints, of colonial societies. As workers who made goods, as servants who helped owners consume, and as objects of trade themselves, slaves kept a coastal world afloat, economically.

Repeated waves of importation meant that African memories and forms of culture were reinvigorated throughout the first several generations in the New World. However, many of the slaves that arrived on the North American mainland did not come directly from Africa, but had already served in the West Indies. African Americans helped create a new Atlantic world, a world of several languages, a world of immigrants and travelers. America was different from England and Africa because it was peopled primarily by willing and unwilling migrants and their children.

These slaves found that any fight against their condition had to take into account the particular nature of American slavery and its variations in different regions. There were several attempts at slave rebellions in the colonial era: in New York in 1712 and 1741, in South Carolina in 1739. But generally, the nature of colonial society, with its relatively small and dispersed population, meant that the struggle against slavery was directed at trying to become more free within the system of slavery itself rather than attempting to overthrow the system. Except for the swamps and Indian country, in the colonial era, there was no free land to which a slave could run away. However, successful fugitives could find a better situation by hiring themselves out to the many white Americans who wanted workers but could not afford (or did not want to buy) slaves. Some slaves worked their way to freedom, or into indentured servitude, by negotiating with their owners. An essential part of the making of American slavery was the making of African-American ways of fighting slavery, of negotiating for some freedom within the system, and of developing their own resources. In the laws passed by colonial assemblies, and in the ways masters tried to keep slaves from running away and then tried to recapture them when they did, we can see how slaves developed strategies that would cause changes in the slave system and hasten its end in some areas of colonial North America. Running away, creating opportunities to interact among themselves, and sometimes plotting violent rebellions all remained important ways of resisting throughout slavery's American history.

Scholars have long debated the extent of slave resistance in the southern states before the Civil War. If we begin our inquiry at the beginnings of American slavery, however, we can see that the institution was always being opposed by the slaves themselves, in ways that changed the nature of what it meant to be a slave—or a master.

## Capture and Transport

Olaudah Equiano (1745–97) was one of the few African-born slaves to write down his memories of being captured and sold. His *Interesting Narrative of the Life of Olaudah Equiano or Gustavus Vassa, the African,* first published in America in 1791, became an important argument against slavery and the slave trade, for it proved to sympathetic whites that Africans, often depicted as unfeeling "savages," were capable of literary writing, as well as deep sorrow at the loss of their families and homes.

In these excerpts, Equiano describes the moment of his capture by African slave traders and some of the events aboard ship as he and other Africans of various tribes sailed westward, after being sold to Europeans. Both passages remind us of the difficult adjustments that slaves had to make. Many, like Equiano, strove to keep their African names and to keep alive the memories of their homelands, although some also served as slaves in Africa before arriving in the New World. Slavery included many different experiences: as Equiano implies, slave life in Africa was less harsh than plantation life for slaves in the Americas. Some artisans and sailors, like Equiano, became true cosmopolitans of the 18th-century Atlantic world, as they performed different tasks for their owners in Africa, in South America, in the Caribbean, on the North American mainland, and on the ships that sailed constantly between those places, transporting goods.

*So large a quantity of tobacco is raised in Maryland and Virginia, that it is one of the greatest sources of revenue to the crown by reason of the taxes which it yields.*

— Jasper Danckaerts, a Dutch traveler in the North American colonies, in his journal, December 1679

*The title page of Olaudah Equiano's* Interesting Narrative *shows the finely dressed author holding a Bible, which emphasizes his status as a learned person and a Christian. Equiano also draws attention on the title page to his identity as an African, thus challenging the colonial stereotype of Africans as "savages" who were incapable of literacy and refinement.*

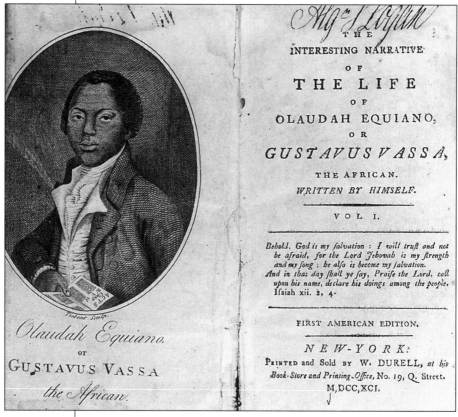

One day, when all our people were gone out to their work as usual, and only I and my sister were left to mind the house, two men and a woman got over our walls, and in a moment seized us both; and, without giving us time to cry out, or to make resistance, they stopped our mouths, and ran off with us into the nearest wood. Here they tied our hands, and continued to carry us as far as they could, till night came on, when we reached a small house . . . . The next morning we left the house, and continued travelling all the day. . . .

The next day proved a day of greater sorrow than I had yet experienced; for my sister and I were then separated, while we lay clasped in each other's arms. It was in vain that we besought them not to part us; she was torn from me, and immediately carried away, while I was left in a state of distraction not to be described. I cried and grieved continually; and for several days did not eat anything but what they forced into my mouth. At length, after many days' travelling, during which I had often changed masters, I got into the hands of a chieftain, in a very pleasant country. This man had two wives and some children, and they all used me extremely well. . . .

I was there, I suppose, about a month, and they at length used to trust me some little distance from the house. . . . I therefore determined to seize the first opportunity of making my escape, and to shape my course for that quarter; for I was quite oppressed and weighed down by grief after my mother and friends; and my love of liberty, ever great, was strengthened by the mortifying circumstance of not daring to eat with the free-born children, although I was mostly their companion. . . .

**Equiano describes the horrors of a slave ship.**

The first object which saluted my eyes when I arrived on the coast was the sea, and a slave ship, which was then riding at anchor, and waiting for its cargo. These filled me with astonishment, that was soon converted into terror. . . . when I was carried on board. . . .

I now saw myself deprived of all chance of returning to my native country, or even the least glimpse of gaining the shore, which I now considered as friendly; and I even wished for my former slavery, in preference of my present situation, which was filled with horrors of every kind, still heighted by my ignorance of what I was to undergo. I was not long suffered to indulge my grief. I was soon put down under the decks, and there I received such a salutation in my nostrils as I had never experienced in my life: so that, with the loathsomeness of the stench, and crying together, I became so sick and low that I was not able to eat, nor had I the least desire to taste anything. I now wished for the last friend, death, to relieve me; but soon, to my grief, two of the white men offered me eatables; and, on my refusing to eat, one of them held me fast by the hands, and laid me across, I think, the windlass, and tied my feet, while the other flogged me severely. I had never experienced anything of this kind before, and although not being used to the water, I naturally feared that element the first time I saw it, yet, nevertheless, could I have got over the nettings, I would have jumped over the side, but I could not; and besides the crew used to watch us very closely who were not chained down to the decks, lest we should leap into the water; and I have seen some

Those negroes make the best slaves that have been slaves in their own country; for they that have been kings and great men are generally lazy, haughty and obstinate; whereas the others are sharper, better humored, and more laborious.

—Hugh Jones, *The Present State of Virginia*, 1724

*This Portuguese slave ship was captured in 1839 by the H.M.S. Scout. At the time of its capture it had a crew of 35 men and 676 slaves on board. Overcrowding and unhealthy conditions resulted in the death of one in six of the Africans transported to the Americas as slaves.*

of these poor African prisoners most severely cut for attempting to do so, and hourly whipped for not eating. This indeed was often the case with myself.

# Early Resistance

**Early in American history, the southern colonies began the process of becoming slave societies—societies whose very existence depended on the labor of slaves. Like their neighbors to the north, colonies such as Virginia began using slaves early in the 17th century, but the slaves remained few in number. It was only later on that Virginia, for example, began to import blacks in large numbers to serve as the primary labor force on its increasingly profitable tobacco plantations.**

**From the beginning, unfree laborers toiled on the farms of North America. More than half of the early immigrants to the mainland were indentured servants, men and women who had sold their labor for a period of years (usually five or seven years) to pay for their passage to America. In the early days, there was not much difference between slaves and indentured servants. Some slaves won their freedom and went on to farm their own land. Eventually, however, the conditions for white workers improved, while those for blacks worsened.**

**There were several reasons for these changes. The supply of white laborers decreased when economic conditions got better in England: as a result, people who wished to buy servants found them more expensive, and better able to demand more rights for themselves. Around the same time, the British Empire won its wars against the Dutch and increased its power on the high seas. British colonists could therefore import slaves from Africa and the West Indies much more cheaply than before. Finally, the authorities in Virginia reacted to a series of uprisings on the part of settlers, servants, and slaves by passing laws designed to keep slaves peaceful. This law of 1680, passed by the Virginia House of Burgesses, is an early example of the "slave codes" that made inequality the official policy of the southern colonies and, later, the southern states.**

*An act for preventing Negroes Insurrections.*

WHEREAS the frequent meeting of considerable numbers of negroe slaves under pretence of feasts and buriall is judged of

TO BE SOLD, on WEDNESDAY 3d AUGUST next,

## By COWPER & TELFAIRS,

A CARGO

Of 170 prime young likely healthy

# GUINEA SLAVES,

Just imported, in the Bark Friends, William Ross Master, directly from Angola.                    Savannah, July 25, 1774.

To be Sold at Private Sale, any Time before the 18th of next Month,

THE PLANTATION, containing one hundred acres, on which the subscriber lives, very pleasantly situated on Savannah River in sight of town.  The terms of sale may be known by applying to
July 21, 1774                              RICHARD WYLLY.

WANTED,

AN OVERSEER thoroughly qualified to undertake the settlement of a River Swamp Plantation on the Alatamaha River.  Any such person, who can bring proper recommendations, may hear of great encouragement by applying to                 NATHANIEL HALL.

THE subscriber being under an absolute necessity of closing his concerns without delay, gives this last publick notice, that all persons indebted to him by bond, note or otherwise, who do not discharge the same by the first day of October next, will find their respective obligations, &c in the hands of an Attorney to be sued for without distinction.  It is hoped those concerned will avail themselves of this notice.
                                            PHILIP BOX.

These advertisements in a 1774 Savannah, Georgia, newspaper show the range of activities that occurred as the colonies developed into slave societies. The colonists imported slaves in large numbers, bought and sold plantations, and hired overseers to manage the growing slave population.

dangerous consequence; for prevention whereof for the future, *Bee it enacted by the kings most excellent majestie by and with the consent of the generall assembly, and it is hereby enacted by the authority aforesaid*, that from and after the publication of this law, it shall not be lawfull for any negroe or other slave to carry or arme himselfe with any club, staffe, gunn, sword or any other weapon of defence or offence, nor to goe or depart from of his masters ground without a certificate from his master, mistris or overseer, and such permission not to be granted but upon perticuler and necessary occasions; and every negroe or slave soe offending not haveing a certificate as aforesaid shalbe sent to the next constable, who is hereby enjoyned and required to give the said negroe twenty lashes on his bare back well layd on, and soe sent home to his said master, mistris or overseer. *And it is further enacted by the authority aforesaid* that if any negroe or other slave shall presume to lift up his hand in opposition against any christian, shall for every such offence, upon due proofe made thereof by the oath of the party before a magistrate, have and receive thirty lashes on his bare back well laid on. *And it is hereby further enacted by the authority aforesaid* that if any negroe or other slave shall absent himself from his masters service and lye hid and lurking in obscure places, comitting injuries to the inhabitants, and shall resist any person or persons that shalby any lawfull authority be imployed to apprehend and take the said

The servants and negroes after they have worn themselves down the whole day, and come home to rest, have yet to grind and pound the grain, which is generally maize [corn], for their masters and all their families as well as themselves, and all the negroes, to eat.

—Jasper Danckaerts's journal entry, December 1679

negroe, that then in case of such resistance, it shalbe lawfull for such person or persons to kill the said negroe or slave soe lying out and resisting, and that this law be once every six months published at the respective county courts and parish churches within this colony.

**As the 1680 law indicates, slaves found many ways to escape their bondage, if often only temporarily. The laws that dictated harsh punishments—and made it illegal for Africans, slave or free, to carry weapons or meet together without prior approval by masters—were formed in response to the resourcefulness of slaves who found ways to increase their autonomy. The "outlying" slaves mentioned in the following Virginia statute of 1691 refer to those who ran away and hid in swamps or other unsettled areas. These slaves, like free blacks, often aided other slaves who ran away, and by their very example they let it be known that slavery could be escaped.**

**Early on, then, the slave system depended on limiting the rights of free Africans as well as those of whites and Indians who aided them. This law made it illegal for whites to marry blacks or Indians, whether they were free or not. It also made it difficult for masters to free their slaves and for freedmen and women to remain, if they wished to remain, in Virginia. Through such measures, the slave societies of the South hoped to—and to a large extent did—keep the races separate. Indeed, they made race itself, aside from wealth or condition of servitude, a key component of social superiority and inferiority.**

*An act for suppressing outlying Slaves.*

WHEREAS many times negroes, mulattoes, and other slaves unlawfully absent themselves from their masters and mistresses service, and lie hid and lurk in obscure places killing hoggs and committing other injuries to the inhabitants of this dominion, for remedy whereof for the future, *Be it enacted by their majesties lieutenant Governour, Councell and Burgesses of this present generall assembly and the authoritie thereof, and it is hereby enacted,* that in all such cases upon intelligence of any such negroes, mulattoes, or other slaves lying out, two of their majesties justices of the peace of that county, whereof one to be of the quorum, where such negroes, mulattoes, or other slave shall be, shall be impowered and commanded, and are hereby impowered and commanded to issue out their warrants directed to the sherrife of the same county to apprehend such negroes, mulattoes, and other slaves, which said sherriffe is hereby likewise required upon all such occasions to raise such and soe many forces from time to time as he shall think convenient and necessary for the effectuall apprehending such negroes, mulattoes and other slaves, and in case any negroes, mulattoes or other slave or slaves lying out as aforesaid shall resist, runaway, or refuse to deliver and surrender him or themselves to any person or persons that shall be by lawfull authority employed to apprehend and take such negroes, mulattoes or other slaves that in such cases it shall and may be lawfull for such person and persons to kill and distroy such negroes, mulattoes, and other slave or slaves by gunn or any otherwaise whatsoever.

*Provided* that where any negroe, mulattoe slave or slaves shall be killed in pursuance of this act, the owner or owners of such negro or mulatto slave shall be paid for such negro or mulatto slave four thousand pounds of tobacco by the publique. And for prevention of that abominable mixture and spurious issue which hereafter may encrease in the dominion, as well by negroes, mulattoes, and Indians intermarrying with English, or other white women, as by their unlawfull accompanying with one another, *Be it enacted by the authoritie aforesaid, and it is hereby enacted*, that for the time to come, whatsoever English or other white man or woman being free shall intermarry with a negroe, mulatto, or Indian man or woman bond or free, shall within three months after such marriage be banished and removed from this dominion forever, and that the justices of each respective countie within this dominion make it their perticular care, that this act be put in effectuall execution. *And be it further enacted by the authoritie aforesaid, and it is hereby enacted*, That if any English woman being free shall have a bastard child by any negro or mulatto, she pay the sume of fifteen pounds sterling, within one moneth after such bastard child [s]hall be born, to the Church wardens of the parish where she shall be delivered of such child, and in default of such payment she shall be taken into the possession of the said Church wardens and disposed of for five yeares, and the said fine of fifteen pounds, or whatever the woman shall be disposed of for, shall be paid, one third part to their majesties for and towards the support of the government and the contingent charges thereof, and one other third part to the use of the parish where the offence is committed, and the other third part to the informer, and that such bastard child be bound out as a servant by the said Church wardens untill

This law passed by the City of New York in 1731 prohibited "any Negro, Mulatto, or Indian slave above the Age of Fourteen Years" from walking the streets of the city at night unaccompanied by their master or without a lantern or candle to illuminate their presence. This law points to the colonists' fear of slaves and the possibility of rebellion, and to the lengths they went to monitor their slaves' movement.

**Mulatto**

A person born of white and black parents. This term was used for lighter-skinned persons of African descent regardless of their parentage.

*City of New-York, ſs.*

# A LAW,

## For Regulating Negroes and Slaves in the Night Time.

BE It Ordained by the Mayor, Recorder, Aldermen and Aſſiſtants of the City of New-York, convened in Common-Council, and it is hereby Ordained by the Authority of the ſame, That from hence-forth no Negro, Mulatto or Indian Slave, above the Age of Fourteen Years, do preſume to be or appear in any of the Streets of this City, on the South-ſide of the Freſh-Water, in the Night time, above an hour after Sun-ſet; And that if any ſuch Negro, Mulatto or Indian Slave or Slaves, as aforeſaid, ſhall be found in any of the Streets of this City, or in any other Place, on the South ſide of the Freſh-Water, in the Night-time, above one hour after Sun-ſet, without a Lanthorn and lighted Candle in it, ſo as the light thereof may be plainly ſeen (and not in company with his, her or their Maſter or Miſtreſs, or ſome White Perſon or White Servant belonging to the Family whoſe Slave he or ſhe is, or in whoſe Service he or ſhe then are) That then and in ſuch caſe it ſhall and may be lawful for any of his Majeſty's Subjects within the ſaid City to apprehend ſuch Slave or Slaves, not having ſuch Lanthorn and Candle, and forth-with carry him, her or them before the Mayor or Recorder, or any one of the Aldermen of the ſaid City (if at a ſeaſonable hour) and if at an unſeaſonable hour, to the Watch-houſe, there to be confined until the next Morning) who are hereby authorized, upon Proof of the Offence, to commit ſuch Slave or Slaves to the common Goal, for ſuch his, her or their Contempt, and there to remain until the Maſter, Miſtreſs or Owner of every ſuch Slave or Slaves, ſhall pay to the Perſon or Perſons who apprehended and committed every ſuch Slave or Slaves, the Sum of *Four Shillings* current Money of *New-York*, for his, her or their pains and Trouble therein, with Reaſonable Charges of Proſecution.

*And be it further Ordained by the Authority aforeſaid,* That every Slave or Slaves that ſhall be convicted of the Offence aforeſaid, before he, ſhe or they be diſcharged out of Cuſtody, ſhall be Whipped at the Publick Whipping-Poſt (not exceeding *Forty Lashes*) if deſired by the Maſter or Owner of ſuch Slave or Slaves.

*Provided always, and it is the intent hereof,* That if two or more Slaves (Not exceeding the Number of Three) be together in any lawful Employ or Labour for the Service of their *Maſter* or *Miſtreſs* (and not otherwiſe) and only one of them have and carry ſuch Lanthorn with a lighted Candle therein, the other Slaves in ſuch Compay not carrying a Lanthorn and lighted Candle, ſhall not be conſtrued and intended to be within the meaning and Penalty of this Law, any thing in this Law contained to the contrary hereof in any wiſe notwithſtanding. *Dated at the City-Hall this Two and Twentieth Day of* April, *in the fourth year of His Majeſty's Reign,* Annoq; Domini 1731.

### By Order of Common Council,

#### Will. Sharpas, Cl.

he or she shall attaine the age of thirty yeares, and in the case such English woman that shall have such bastard child be a servant, she shall be sold by the said Church wardens (after her time is expired that she ought by law to serve her master) for five yeares, and the money she shall be sold for divided as is before appointed, and the child to serve as aforesaid.

And forasmuch as great inconveniences my happen to this country by the setting of negroes and mulattoes free, by their either entertaining negro slaves from their masters service, or receiveing stolen goods, or being grown old bringing a charge upon the country; for prevention thereof, *Be it enacted by the authority aforesaid, and it is hereby enacted,* That no negro or mulatto be after the end of this present session of assembly set free by any person or persons whatsoever, unless such person or persons, their heires, executors or administrators pay for the transportation of such negro or negroes out of the countrey within six moneths after such setting them free, upon penalty of paying of tenn pounds sterling to the Church wardens of the parish where such person shall dwell with, which money, or so much thereof as shall be necessary, the said Church wardens are to cause the said negro or mulattoe to be transported out of the countrey, and the remainder of the said money to imploy to the use of the poor of the parish.

**The towns of colonial America were centers of trade. People came from all over the county and beyond to buy or swap for what they needed or to sell the goods they had grown or made. Some slaves took advantage of the marketplace to engage in their own trading, often of crops they had grown on their own, in lots given to them for producing their own food.**

**This decree of municipal law from the town records of Wilmington, North Carolina, reveals the frustration felt by some slave owners whose slaves were using the town market to their own ends. Like the previous documents, it also indicates that whites found gatherings of Africans to be threatening and went to surprising lengths to prevent such meetings.**

[January 22, 1772]
AND WHEREAS, many white People within this Town, have long practised dealing with Negroes, to the great Detriment as well of their owners as to the Community in general; It is therefore,

ORDERED, That no white person or persons, hereafter, shall on any pretence whatever, hire any Negro or Negroes, such Negroe not having a Ticket from his or her owner or Overseer, granting leave to such Negroe or Negroes to hire him, her or themselves; Nor shall any white Person whatever on any pretense, presume to deal, Trade or Traffic with any Slave or Slaves for any matter or thing whatever, without a Ticket or Tickets from the Master, Mistress or Overseer of such Slave or Slaves, particularly expressing the same, under the Penalty of Forty Shillings Procl. [proclamation, or official] Money.

*Every freeman of Carolina, shall have absolute power and authority over his negro slaves, of what opinion or religion soever.*

—The Fundamental Constitutions of the Carolinas, drawn up by British philosopher John Locke, 1669

And to prevent Riotting and Disturbances that often happen among the Negroes in the s[ai]d Town, It is,. . .

ORDERED, That if any number of slaves exceeding Three, shall, after the Tenth day of February next, be seen together in the Streets, Alleys, Vacant Lots, House, Out Houses or other Parts within this Town, or the limits thereof, Playing, Rioting or Caballing on the Sabath Day, or in the Night time of that day, or in the Night time of any other day, whereby the Inhabitants or any of them may be disturbed or Mollested, the slave or slaves so offending shall be apprehended and whipped at the discretion of any one or more of the Commissioners.

**Slaves who worked in the marketplace often promoted their own ventures, to the dismay of their owners. Evan Powel posted this advertisement in the *Pennsylvania Gazette*, the Philadelphia newspaper edited by Benjamin Franklin, on March 5, 1745. It is revealing that the master does not specify whether Bess was a slave or an indentured servant. Both slaves and servants were doing the kinds of work and selling at which Bess, apparently, succeeded.**

These are to give Notice, that whereas Molatto Bess, who used to go about selling Cakes, has been often complained of to her Master for borrowing of Money and taking up Goods upon Trust in her Master's Name, and unknown either to her Master or Mistress; these are therefore requesting, that no Person upon what Pretence soever, may hereafter trust her with either Money or Goods, or entertain her in their Houses, upon their Peril.

## Slaves' Lives in the Colonies

**By the late 18th century, African Americans had developed their own culture from a fusion of African and European elements. Nicholas Cresswell, a young English immigrant to Maryland who traveled in the colonies, reveals his own prejudices when he calls slaves' dances and music "rude" and "grotesque." Like many whites, he was probably more than a little uncomfortable seeing and hearing blacks discussing their treatment as unjust and making fun of whites.**

*Sunday, May 29th, 1774.* . . . Mr. Bayley and I went to see a Negro Ball. Sundays being the only days these poor creatures have to

*This painting from about 1800 by an unknown artist offers a unique glimpse into slaves' independent culture. The plantation house is far distant and the slaves, who are attired with elements of African costume, are engrossed in their music and dance. Some scholars believe that the scene depicts the marriage celebration of the couple on the right.*

themselves, they generally meet together and amuse themselves with Dancing to the Banjo. This musical instrument (if it may be so called) is made of a Gourd something in the imitation of a Guitar, with only four strings and played with the fingers in the same manner. Some of them sing to it, which is very droll music indeed. In their songs they generally relate the usage they have received from their Masters or Mistresses in a very satirical stile and manner. Their poetry is like the Music—Rude and uncultivated. Their Dancing is most violent exercise, but so irregular and grotesque. I am not able to describe it. They all appear to be exceedingly happy at these merrymakings and seem as if they had forgot or were not sensible of their miserable condition.

**William Moraley, an indentured servant, wrote about his trip to the middle colonies after his return to England in the early 1740s. In his book, *The Infortunate* (1743), Moraley described a slave system in Pennsylvania that, although it may not have been a "slave society," certainly had many of the same features that marked slavery further south. In both cases, it seems, the labor of Africans came to be seen as "necessary," and the violent treatment of slaves was justified in similar ways. Indeed, as Moraley contends, slave labor helped the American colonies, especially the middle colonies, become known all over the Europe as "the best poor man's country"—that is, the best place for ordinary, white people to get work or their own land (although Moraley himself had difficulties making a living in the New World).**

**In Pennsylvania as well as in other colonies, slaves developed their own customs, including family institutions,**

within the slave system. Whites, like Moraley, knew that these institutions—slave marriage, garden plots, Sundays off—helped maintain slavery itself by reducing the slaves' inclination to run away. They also knew, as Moraley admitted, that slaves faced violence regularly and were treated cruelly. And like Moraley, whites justified that cruelty as unavoidable; without it, the slaves would not work for their masters—or worse, they might become violent themselves and rebel.

*This indentured servant's contract from 1698 indicates that 15-year-old Thomas will work as an unpaid servant for four years on a Virginia plantation to pay for his passage to the colonies. Unlike captured Africans who also may have worked at this Virginia plantation, Thomas willingly signed this agreement to serve his masters and, in 1702, was free to leave.*

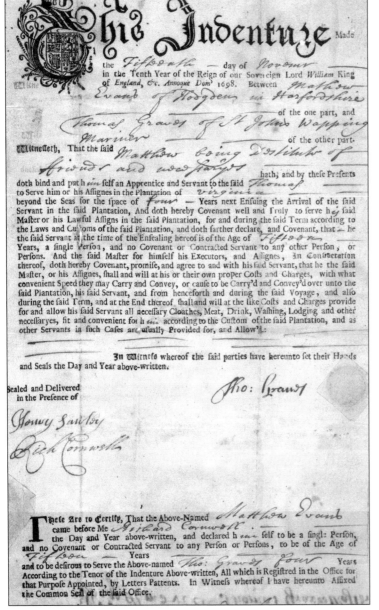

At the first Peopling [of] these Colonies, there was a Necessity of employing a great Number of Hands, for the clearing the Land, being over-grown with Wood for some Hundred of Miles; to which Intent, the first Settlers not being sufficient of themselves to improve those Lands, were not only obliged to purchase a great Number of *English* Servants to assist them, to whom they granted great Immunities and at the Expiration of their Servitude, Land was given to encourage them to continue there; but were likewise obliged to purchase Multitudes of Negro Slaves from *Africa*, by which Means they are become the richest Farmers in the World, paying no Rent, nor giving Wages either to purchased Servants or Negro Slaves; so that instead of finding the Planter Rack-rented, as the *English* Farmer, you will taste of their Liberty, they living in Affluence and Plenty.

The Condition of the Negroes is very bad, by reason of the Severity of the Laws, there being no Laws made in Favour of these unhap[p]y Wretches: For the least Trespass, they undergo the severest Punishment; but their Masters make them some amends, by suffering them to marry, which makes them easier, and often prevents their running away. The Consequence of their marrying is this, all their Posterity are Slaves

without Redemption; and it is in vain to attempt an Escape, tho'
they often endeavour it; for the Laws against them are so severe,
that being caught after running away, they are unmercifully
whipped; and if they die under the Discipline, their Masters suffer
no Punishment, there being no Law against murdering them. So if
one Man kills another's Slave, he is only obliged to pay his Value
to the Master, besides Damages that may accrue for the Loss of
him in his Business.

The Masters generally allow them a Piece of Ground, with
Materials for improving it. The Time of working for themselves, is
*Sundays*, when they raise on their own Account divers Sort of
Corn and Grain, and sell it in the Markets. They buy with the
Money Cloaths for themselves and Wives; as for the Children,
they belong to the Wives Master, who bring them up; so the Negro
need fear no Expense, his Business being to get them for his
Master's use, who is tender of them as his own Children. On
*Sundays* in the evening they converse with their Wives, and drink
Rum, or Bumbo, and smoak Tobacco, and the next Morning return
to their Master's Labour.

They are seldom made free, for fear of being burthensome to
the Provinces, there being a Law, that no Master shall manumise
them, unless he gives Security they shall not be thrown upon the
Province, by settling Land on them for their Support.

Their Marriages are diverting; for when the Day is appointed
for the Solemnization, Notice is given to all the Negroes and their
Wives to be ready. The Masters of the new Couple provide hand-
somely for the Entertainment of the Company. The Inhabi-tants
generally grace the Nuptials with their Presence, when all Sorts of
the best Provisions are to be met with. They chuse some
*Englishman* to read the Marriage Ceremony out of the Common
Prayer Book; after which they sing and dance and drink till they
get drunk. Then a Negro goes about the Company and collects
Money for the Use of the Person who marry'd them, which is laid
out in a Handker-chief, and presented to him.

This is the only free Day they have, except Sundays, throughout the whole Course of their Lives, for then they banish from
them all Thoughts of the Wretchedness of their Condition. The
Day being over, they return to their Slavery. I have often heard
them say, they did not think God made them Slaves, any more
than other Men, and wondered that Christians, especially
*Englishmen*, should use them so barbarously. But there is a Necessity
of using them hardly, being of an obdurate, stubborn Disposition;
and when they have it in their Power to rebel, are extremely cruel.

**Manumise**

To make free in a
legal document.

# Rebels and Runaways

**Sometimes slaves did rebel. Indeed, American slaves took up arms often enough to make their masters extremely nervous. In 1712, a slave rebellion struck New York City. Twenty-nine years later, when a rash of suspicious fires spread through the city, local whites were quick to blame the slave population. Even more blacks were tried and executed as a result of the 1741 scare than perished after the failed revolt described below by Robert Hunter, the royal governor of New York, in a letter to the London Board of Trade.**

**Native Africans, recently imported, took the lead in the New York uprising of 1712. This pattern repeated itself throughout the 18th century, as in the Stono Rebellion outside Charleston, South Carolina, in 1739. The ambush style of warfare that the New York rebels chose perhaps reveals a strategy more appropriate to these slaves' African homelands than to a port city like New York with its own armed fortress.**

I must now give your Lordships an account of a bloody conspiracy of some of the slaves of this place, to destroy as many of the Inhabitants as they could, It was put in execution in this manner, when they had resolved to revenge themselves for some hard usage, they apprehended to have received from their masters (for I can find no other cause) they agreed to meet in the orchard of Mr. Crook the middle of the Town, some provided with fire arms, some with swords and others with knives and hatchets, this was the sixth day of April, the time of meeting was about twelve or one o'clock in the night, when about three and twenty of them were got together, one coffee and negroe slave to one Vantilburgh set fire to an out house of his Masters, and then repairing to the place where the rest were they all sallyed out together [with] their arm's and marched to the fire, by this time the noise of fire spreeding through the town, the people began to flock to it upon the approach of severall the slaves fired and killed them, the noise of the guns gave the allarm, and some escaping their shot soon published the cause of the fire, which was the reason, that not above nine Christians were killed, and about five or six wounded, upon the first notice which was very soon after the mischeif was begun, I order'd a detachment from the fort under a proper officer to march against them, but the slaves made their retreat into the woods, by the favour of the night, having ordered centries the next day in the most proper places on the Island to [prevent] their

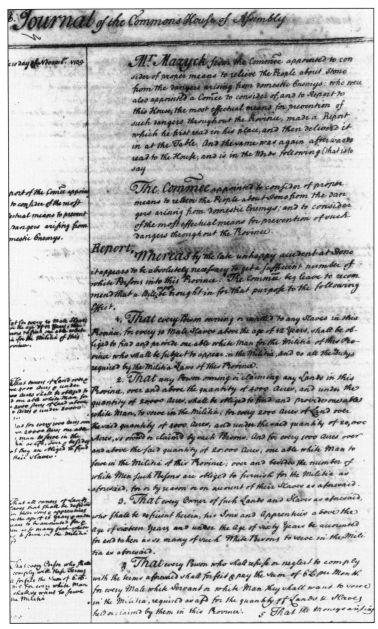

The 1739 Stono Rebellion in South Carolina was a violent bid for freedom by a group of slaves that resulted in the provisions recorded here in the South Carolina Assembly Journal. To protect themselves from "Domestic Enemies," the assembly obligated land and slave owners to provide white men for the state militia in proportion to their number of male slaves or acres of land. Colonists who failed to supply men for the militia would be subject to fines.

escape, I caused the day following the Militia of this town and of the county of west Chester to drive the Island, and by this means and strict searches in the town, we found all that put the design in execution, six of these having first laid violent hands upon themselves, the rest were forthwith brought to their tryal before ye Justices of this place who are authorized by Act of Assembly, to hold a Court in such cases, In that Court were twenty seven condemned whereof twenty one were executed, one being a woman with child, her execution by that meanes suspended, some were burnt others hanged, one broke on the wheele, and one hung a live in chains in the town, so that there has been the most exemplary punishment inflicted that could be possibly thought of, and which only this act of assembly could Justify.

**Much more often than rebelling, slaves chose to run away. This was by far the preferred strategy of American-born slaves, who could use their knowledge of the countryside, and their relationships with other blacks and whites, to evade the slave system temporarily or even permanently.**

**By the 1730s, when newspapers began to appear in most of the colonies, masters took out advertisements for their runaway slaves. These ads tell us much about the resourcefulness of African Americans, and how highly they were valued by their masters. This advertisement, for example, which appeared in the *Pennsylvania Gazette* on March 11, 1731, reminds us that some slaves worked as artisans and as laborers in the era's small factories, as well as on farms and in white households. It also reminds us that slaves not only ran away from whites but toward other blacks. John England strongly suspected that his slave, Jack, might be found where he had previously lived, in New Castle, Delaware.**

RUN away the 27th of *February* from *John England* and Company, at *Principle* Iron Works, a Negro Man named *Jack,* formerly belonging

*In this advertisement from the March 8, 1773,* South Carolina Gazette *John Allwood offers for sale his "negro fellows" who are trained painters and who have "transacted the Whole of his Business without any hired Assistance." During the colonial period it was not uncommon for slaves to be trained artisans such as blacksmiths, carpenters, and, in this case, painters, and to perform important household tasks, as did Allwood's "House-Wench," or female slave. Skilled slaves had greater mobility than field workers and perhaps the chance of earning their freedom.*

The SUBSCRIBER,
Intending to leave the Province in APRIL next,
*WILL DISPOSE OF*
His NEGRO FELLOWS, *Painters,*
On WEDNESDAY *the* Seventh *of April* next,
At *his Yard in* Queen-Street, *directly opposite Mr.* CANNON's.

AS to their Abilities, he thinks them evident, they having transacted the Whole of his Business, without any hired Assistance; and he has taken no little Pains in initiating them in the true Principles of their Profession.
*LIKEWISE,*
A good HOUSE-WENCH,
Who can wash and iron exceeding well, and is a tolerable Cook.

He has also a few well-painted Pictures to dispose of; some good Prints, framed and glazed; with a little Houshold-Furniture.——The Conditions will be made known on the Day of Sale.
\*\*\* He begs those to whom he is indebted to send in their Accompts for Payment;——and requests the Favour of those who are indebted to him, to discharge their Accompts; by which Means he hopes to give his Creditors general Satisfaction.
JOHN ALLWOOD.

to sir *William Keith*, Bart at his Works in *New-Castle* County: He is an elderly Man, speaks thick, and generally pretty Sawcy; is a Carpenter by Trade, and has a Wife in *New-Castle* County. Whoever secures him, so as his Master may have him again, shall have *Five Pounds* Reward, and reasonable Charges paid, by

John England.

**Some slaves used their ambiguous racial identity to their advantage. Mulattoes, or people of mixed black and white backgrounds, were more likely than native-born Africans or darker-skinned creoles (mixed-race people born in the colonies) to be free; they also could, at times, pass for white. And because African Americans were a common sight aboard sailing ships and along the harbors of early America, wartime provided additional opportunities for a change of status. The runaway slave described in the advertisement below sought to join the British and American forces during the Seven Years' War.**

New-York, July 10, 1760

RUN away from DENNIS HICKS, of Philipsburgh, in Westchester County, and Province of New-York, A Mulatto Man Slave, named Bill, about 20 Years of Age, has a long sharp Nose, with a black Mole on the right Side of his Face, near his Nose, has very large Ears, speaks good English, and pretends to be free, and can read and write well; says he has a White Mother, and was born in New-England: He is of a middle Size, and has a thin Visage, with his Hair cut off. All Persons are forbid to harbour him, and all Masters of Vessels are forbid to carry him off, as they will answer it at their Peril. TWENTY-FIVE POUNDS Reward for securing him in any Goal, or bringing him to me, so that I may have him again, and reasonable Charges, paid by DENNIS HICKS.

N.B. This Fellow was advertised in the New-York Papers the 5th of June, and in New-Haven the 11th of June, 1759; was afterwards taken up in Waterbury, and was put into Litchfield Goal, from thence he was brought to Bedford, and there made his Escape from his Master again. Those who apprehend him, are desired to secure him in Irons. He was taken up by Moses Foot, of North-Waterbury, in New-England. It is likely he will change his Cloaths, as he did before. The Mole above mentioned is something long.

*By Information he was in Morris County, in the Jerseys all the Winter, and said he would enter into the Provincial Service.

Peter Salem, the Colored American, at Bunker Hill. Page 21

*Chapter Two*

# The African-American Revolution

The American Revolution shook the foundations of colonial society—but not always in ways that the revolutionaries intended. Many, perhaps most, of those who supported the rebellion did so in the hope that things would stay the same, or at least return to the recent past, when the British government did not heavily tax the Americans and, for the most part, let the colonists run their own affairs. To protest new taxes and new rules, the colonists drew upon the ideas of "natural" rights—freedoms that all people deserved from birth—and "ancient" liberties that had been fought for throughout the history of England. For this reason, the colonists called themselves Whigs, in honor of the party in British politics they associated with the tradition of preserving freedom and liberty.

But once the issue of "liberty" and freedom had been raised, as it had by the 1760s, it became difficult, if not impossible, to prevent oppressed groups in the colonies from taking up the call for liberty on their own behalf. Soon after the Sons of Liberty in Charleston, South Carolina, protested the British Parliament's tax on paper (the Stamp Act) by flying a British flag with the word "Liberty" written in large letters, a group of slaves was heard shouting "Liberty" in the street. At the time, Charleston had just experienced one of its periodic rumors of a slave insurrection. In America, then, liberty—and rebellion—was a two-way street. One person's liberty was another's rebellious overthrow of law. The white American revolutionaries acknowledged as much when they repeatedly compared their treatment by the British to slavery.

The war itself, once it began with the "shot heard 'round the world" at Concord in 1775, was actually a four-way affair, at the very least. Just as the Rebels, or Whigs (who called themselves the Patriots)

*This illustration from William Cooper Nell's 1855 book,* Colored Patriots of the American Revolution, *celebrates the role African-American soldiers played in the war. Peter Salem, who fought in the battles at Bunker Hill, Saratoga, and Stony Point, was freed by his master so he could fight for the Patriots during the Revolutionary War.*

competed with the Tories (or Loyalists) for the support of the rest of the colonists, so did both groups need to keep Indians and slaves from fighting for the other side. Especially in the South— the area with the greatest number of slaves—the Revolution became a civil war, as colonists slew each other with the help of the British army and some Indian tribes (who fought for the Tories) and, eventually, the French (on the side of the Patriots). Promised freedom by both sides, African Americans fought for both. And the disorders of war quickly enabled blacks to fight for themselves, by running away.

Ultimately, the American Revolution became an African-American revolution as well, when blacks escaped slavery in large numbers. One-third of Georgia's slaves became free; the black population of South Carolina declined by about 25 percent. Those who survived the war helped to establish free black communities in the South, in northern towns, and in parts of Canada. These Americans—former slaves—had gained independence, but would they really have liberty? And what about those who remained enslaved after the final American victory at Yorktown? The struggle against slavery took new forms during the Revolution, and the system would never be the same afterward.

## Liberty for All?

**By the early 1770s, slaves in New England—the center of colonial resistance to Great Britain—had picked up on the rhetoric of "liberty" and "slavery" being employed by whites. Petitioning the courts and legislatures, much as colonists petitioned the British government, they turned this rhetoric to their own advantage. Blacks claimed that colonists who fought for liberty from Britain should also oppose slavery at home. Such arguments had real effects: in a 1783 judicial decision, Massachusetts abolished slavery. In 1773, four Massachusetts slaves circulated this petition to members of the colony's legislature.**

Boston, April 20th, 1773.
Sir, The efforts made by the legislative of this province in their last sessions to free themselves from slavery, gave us, who are in that deplorable state, a high degree of satisfaction. We expect great things from men who have made such a noble stand against the designs of their *fellow-men* to enslave them. We cannot but wish and hope Sir, that you will have the same grand object, we mean civil

Whilst we are spilling our blood and exhausting our treasure in defence of our own liberty, it would not perhaps be amiss to turn our eyes towards those of our fellow-men who are now groaning in bondage under us. We say "all men are equally entitled to liberty and the pursuit of happiness;" but are we willing to grant this liberty to all men?

—John Cooper, *New Jersey Gazette*, September 20, 1780

and religious liberty, in view in your next session. The divine spirit of *freedom,* seems to fire every humane breast on this continent, except such as are bribed to assist in executing the execrable plan.

We are very sensible that it would be highly detrimental to our present masters, if we were allowed to demand all that of *right* belongs to us for past services; this we disclaim. Even the *Spaniards,* who have not those sublime ideas of freedom that English men have, are conscious that they have no right to all the services of their fellow-men, we mean the *Africans,* whom they have purchased with their money; therefore they allow them one day in a week to work for themselves, to enable them to earn money to purchase the residue of their time, which they have a right to demand such portions as they are able to pay for (a due appraizement of their services being first made, which always stands at the purchase money.) We do not pretend to dictate to you Sir, or to the honorable Assembly, of which you are a member: We acknowledge our obligations to you for what you have already done, but as the people of this province seem to be actuated by the principles of equity and justice, we cannot but expect your house will again take our deplorable case into serious consideration, and give us that ample relief which, *as men,* we have a natural right to.

But since the wise and righteous governor of the universe, has permitted our fellow men to make us slaves, we bow in submission to him, and determine to behave in such a manner, as that we may have reason to expect the divine approbation of, and assistance in, our peacable and lawful attempts to gain our freedom.

We are willing to submit to such regulations and laws, as may be made relative to us, until we leave the province, which we determine to do as soon as we can from our joynt labours procure money to transport ourselves to some part of the coast of *Africa,* where we propose a settlement. We are very desirous that you should have instructions relative to us, from your town, therefore

Abigail Adams wrote to her husband John, one of the Founding Fathers, on September 22, 1774, to express her concern over "the iniquitous scheme . . . to fight for ourselves for what we are daily robbing and plundering from those who have as good a right to freedom as we have." As African Americans recognized the hypocrisy of slave owners fighting for an end to tyranny so did some of the more enlightened colonists.

## Maintaining the King's Government

*The patriot Committee of Safety in New Bern, North Carolina, circulated a letter written by the royal governor, John Martin, on June 24, 1775, to Lewis H. DeRossett, a member of the colony's legislature, in which the governor threatened to enlist slaves to fight against their masters.*

"[N]othing could ever justify the design, falsely imputed to me, of giving encouragement to the negroes, but the actual and declared rebellion of the King's subjects, and the failure of all others means to maintain the King's Government."

we pray you to communicate this letter to them, and ask this favor for us.

In behalf of our fellow slaves in this province, And by order of their Committee.

Peter Bestes,
Sambo Freeman,
Felix Holbrook,
Chester Joie.

For the Representative of the town of Thompson.

**Of all the slaves and free blacks who took up the pen to fight slavery during the Revolutionary era, none earned more fame than Phillis Wheatley. A slave born in Africa during the mid-1750s, she amazed her Boston owners, the Wheatleys, with her intellectual abilities and her sincere conversion to Christianity. At a time when higher education was pursued primarily by boys and men, religion justified study for women as well. When Phillis began to write poetry in 1767, her poems were devotional meditations in the Puritan tradition. But her religious convictions did not prevent her from writing political poetry. By the 1770s, she was writing poems celebrating the American Patriots—and some of these have a distinctly antiracist message.**

**The very fact that Wheatley could write poetry challenged assumptions that Africans were intellectually inferior—assumptions that were being used to argue against freeing the slaves. The publication of Wheatley's *Poems on Various Subjects, Religious and Moral* (1773) was itself an antislavery action. The book even included a portrait of Wheatley, to make sure that readers knew her skin was dark.**

**The following two poems are good examples of how Wheatley used poetry, and in particular a kind of poetic gratitude to whites, to argue in favor of black equality. In the first poem, Wheatley depicts Africa as a "pagan land" where she lived in ignorance of Christian doctrines; in America she has been saved—which proves that Africans can be as good, as holy or "refined," as white Europeans.**

## On being brought from AFRICA to AMERICA.

'TWAS mercy brought me from my *Pagan* land,
Taught my benighted soul to understand
That there's a God, that there's a *Saviour* too;
Once I redemption neither sought nor knew.

Some view our sable race with scornful eye,
"Their colour is a diabolic die."
Remember, *Christians*, *Negroes*, black as *Cain*,
May be refin'd, and join th' angelic train.

**Wheatley's second poem praises the earl of Dartmouth, a British aristocrat who had supported the publication of her poems and who had just been appointed to a high cabinet position where he would be responsible for policy toward the colonies. Like other Bostonians, Wheatley was hoping that Dartmouth would reverse the policies that had caused so much discontent in America. But in predicting a new birth of liberty, she explains that, as a slave taken from Africa, she understands how terrible is its opposite, tyranny. Wishing that New England never be enslaved, Wheatley proved her patriotism and raised doubts about how her own condition could be reconciled with American freedom.**

## To the Right Honourable WILLIAM, Earl of DARTMOUTH, His Majesty's Principal, Secretary of State for North America, &c.

HAIL, happy day, when, smiling like the morn,
Fair *Freedom* rose *New-England* to adorn:
The northern clime beneath her genial ray,
*Dartmouth*, congratulates thy blissful sway:
Elate with hope her race no longer mourns,
Each soul expands, each grateful bosom burns,
While in thine hand with pleasure we behold
The silken reins, and *Freedom's* charms unfold.
Long lost to realms beneath the northern skies
She shines supreme, while hated *faction* dies:
Soon as appear'd the *Goddess* long desir'd,
Sick at the view, the languish'd and expir'd;
Thus from the splendors of the morning light
The owl in sadness seeks the caves of night.

  No more, *America*, in mournful strain
Of wrongs, and grievance unredress'd complain,
No longer shalt thou dread the iron chain,
Which wanton *Tyranny* with lawless hand
Had made, and with it meant t' enslave the land.

  Should you, my lord, while you peruse my song,
Wonder from whence my love of *Freedom* sprung,
Whence flow these wishes for the common good,
By feeling hearts alone best understood,

## Poems from a Slave

*The following preface appeared in the first edition of Phillis Wheatley's* Poems *in 1773.*

We whose Names are underwriten, do assure the World, that the Poems specified in the following Page, were (as we verily believe) written by Phillis, a young Negro Girl, who was but a few Years since, brought an uncultivated Barbarian from *Africa*, and has ever since been, and is, under the Disadvantage of serving as a Slave in a Family in this Town. She has been examined by some of the best Judges, and is thought qualified to write them.

*Phillis Wheatley pictured in the frontispiece to her poems appears to be in the act of composing verse. With this image and the title of her book, Wheatley directly challenged the argument that blacks were incapable of intellectual thought and moral reasoning, which was used to justify slavery.*

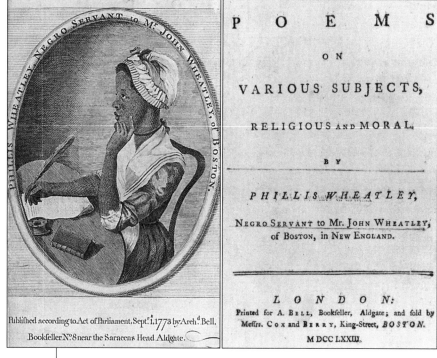

I, young in life, by seeming cruel fate
Was snatch'd from *Afric's* fancy'd happy seat:
What pangs excruciating must molest,
What sorrows labour in my parent's breast?
Steel'd was that soul and by no misery mov'd
That from a father seiz'd his babe belov'd:
Such, such my case. And can I then but pray
Others may never feel tyrannic sway?

    For favours past, great Sir, our thanks are due,
And thee we ask thy favours to renew,
Since in thy pow'r, as in thy will before,
To sooth the griefs, which thou did'st once deplore.
May heav'nly grace the sacred sanction give
To all thy works, and thou for ever live
Not only on the wings of fleeting *Fame*,
Though praise immortal crowns the patriot's name,
But to conduct to heav'ns refulgent fame,
May fiery coursers sweep th' ethereal plain,
And bear thee upwards to that blest abode,
Where, like the prophet, thou shalt find thy God.

**During the early years of the Patriots' resistance to Britain, local committees took responsibility for maintaining boycotts against British goods. The minutes of the town com-**

mittee meeting in Shrewsbury, New Jersey, reveal that many Patriots feared not just the loss of their liberties but also the loss of their slaves. African Americans who met at licensed or unlicensed taverns, like those mentioned below, were doing precisely what the Patriots did to plan their own activities.

[October 16, 1775]

Whereas the Meeting togather of Servants Negros and other Disorderly Persons at Unli[c]enced Taverns and other Bad Houses is attended with Great Mischiefs and Dammage not only to the Masters But to all the Neighbourhood and may Be of more fatal and pernicious Consequence to the Community in General— Therefore in Order that the penaltys of the Law may Be More Duly Inflicted on all Such Offenders, Resolved that the Collonell Shall order a party or parties of the M[i]litia to Attend to Such Suspected places at proper times to Search for and to Apprehend all Such transgressors of the Law.

# Lord Dunmore and the Promise of Freedom

**As soon as the war for independence began, it undermined slavery. Rumors that the British would employ blacks to subdue rebellious whites were circulated in London and at home, from Virginia to South Carolina. The actual taking up of arms by the Royal forces encouraged slaves to run away. The army commanded by Lord Dunmore, the Royal governor of Virginia, became the first refuge of these African Americans who hoped, by serving the Crown (or just by escaping their masters), to gain permanent freedom. Runaways like Charles, described in the advertisement below, certainly gave Lord Dunmore the idea to officially encourage runaways to leave their masters.**

AQUIA, Stafford county, *November 8, 1775.*
RAN off last night from the subscriber, a negro man named CHARLES, who is a very shrewd, sensible fellow, and can both read and write; and as he always has waited upon me, he must be well known through most parts of *Virginia* and *Maryland.* He is very black, has a large nose, and is about 5 feet 8 or 10 inches high. He took a variety of clothes, which I cannot well particularize, stole several of my shirts, a pair of new saddle bags, and two mares, one a darkish, the other a light bay, with a blaze

**Militia**
Armed forces staffed by local citizens.

*To every Negro who shall desert the Rebel Standard, full security to follow within these Lines, any Occupation which he shall think proper.*
—General Sir Henry Clinton, commander in chief of the British forces, 1779

and white feet, and about 3 years old. From the many circumstances, there is reason to believe he intends an attempt to get to lord Dunmore; and as I have reason to believe his design of going off was long premeditated, and that he has gone off with some accomplice, I am apprehensive he may prove daring and resolute, if endeavered to be taken. His elopement was from no cause of complaint, or dread of whipping (for he has always been remarkably indulged, indeed too much so) but from a determined resolution to get liberty, as he conceived, by flying to lord Dunmore. I will give FIVE POUNDS to any person who secures him, and the mares, so that I get them again.

ROBERT BRENT

**Dunmore's carefully worded proclamation of November 1775 freed only the slaves of Rebel masters and only those who actually joined the British forces. Dunmore did not want to encourage wholesale slave rebellion, which would have angered loyal Virginian slaveholders. But he did want to make the Rebels as vulnerable as possible. This vulnerability, especially given the large number of southern slaves (in some places more than half of the population), contributed to the Crown's "southern strategy" for winning the war. It certainly helped make the Revolution a bloody, destructive contest in places like South Carolina and Georgia. It also encouraged the Rebels themselves to enroll free blacks and slaves in their armed forces—and to promise some of the slaves freedom if they served for the duration of the war.**

By His Excellency the Right Honorable JOHN Earl of DUNMORE, His MAJESTY's Lieutenant and Governor General of the Colony and Dominion of VIRGINIA, and Vice Admiral of the same

A PROCLAMATION.

AS I have ever entertained Hopes, that an Accomadation might have taken Place between Great Britain and this Colony, without being compelled by my Duty on this most disagreeable but now absolutely necessary Step, rendered so by a Body of armed Men unlawfully assembled, firing on His Majesty's Tenders, and the formation of an Army, and that Army now on their March to attack his Majesty's Troops and destroy the well disposed Subjects of this Colony. To defeat such reasonable Purposes, and that all such Traitors, and their Abettors, may be brought to Justice, and

**Tender**

A small boat sent out from a larger ship.

that the Peace, and good Order of this Colony may be again restored, which the ordinary Course of the Civil Law is unable to effect; I have thought fit to issue this my Proclamation, hereby declaring, that until the aforesaid good Purposes can be obtained, I do in Virtue of the Power and Authority to ME given, by His Majesty, determine to execute Martial Law, and cause the same to be executed through this Colony and to that the Peace and good Order may the sooner be restored, I do require every Person capable of bearing Arms, to resort to His Majesty's STANDARD, or to be looked upon as Traitors to His Majesty's Crown and Government, and thereby become liable to the Penalty the Law inflicts upon such Offences; such as forfeiture of Life, confiscation of Lands, &c. &c. And I do hereby further declare all indentured Servants, Negroes, or others, (appertaining to Rebels,) free that are able and willing to bear Arms, they joining His Majesty's Troops as soon as may be, for the more speedily reducing this Colony to a proper Sense of their Duty, to His Majesty's Crown and Dignity. I do further order, and require, all His Majesty's Liege Subjects, to retain their Quitrents, or any other Taxes due or that may become due, in their own Custody, till such Time as Peace may be again restored to this at present most unhappy Country, or demanded of them for their former salutary Purposes, by Officers properly authorized to recieve the fame.

GIVEN under my Hand on the boat, the Ship WILLIAM, in NORFOLK, the 7th Day of NOVEMBER, in the sixteenth Year of His Majesty's Reign.
     DUNMORE
     (God save the KING.)

**The fears of Virginia slaveholders were quickly realized. This 1775 letter from Edmund Pendleton to Richard Henry Lee describes a skirmish in the countryside in which master and slave fought each other under the banners of the British and the Virginia Rebels. Pendleton and Lee were wealthy planters and leaders in Virginia politics.**

Eight companies, with some baggage, had passed the river at *Jamestown*, and were waiting at *Cobham* for the remainder with Colonel *Woodford*, who were obliged by the navy to go up the river to pass, and did not get over till *Sunday* sen'night. In the mean time, Colonel *Joseph Hutchings*, and some others in *Princess Anne*, raised about one hundred and seventy men, and were marching to

The Earl of Dunmore, whose proclamation freed blacks who served the Loyalist army, is portrayed in his family's traditional Scottish garb. Dunmore enjoyed a brief popularity after leading a war against some of Virginia's neighboring Indians, but quickly lost the support of the planters when he threatened to put down colonial resistance with the help of slaves.

meet and join *Woodford's* corps. The Governour, hearing of this, marched out with three hundred and fifty soldiers, tories and slaves, to *Kemp's Landing*, and after setting up his standard, and issuing his proclamation, declaring all persons Rebels who took up arms for the country, and inviting all slaves, servants, and apprentices, to come to him and receive arms, he proceeded to intercept *Hutchings* and his party, upon whom he came by surprise, but received, it seems, so warm a fire, that the ragamuffins gave way, they were however rallied, on discovering that two companies of our militia gave way, and left *Hutchings* and Dr. *Reid* with a volunteer company, who maintained their ground bravely, till they were overcome by numbers, and took shelter in a swamp. The slaves were sent in pursuit of them; and one of Colonel *Hutching's* own, with another, found him. On their approach, he discharged his pistol at his slave, but missed him, and was taken by them after receiving a wound in his face with a sword. The numbers taken or killed, on either side, is not ascertained. It is said the Governour went to Dr. *Reid's* shop, and after taking the medicines and dressings necessary for his wounded men, broke all the others to pieces. Letters mention that slaves flock to him in abundance, but I hope it is magnified.

# The Declaration of Independence and the Question of Slavery

**By 1776, the slaves' claim for liberty had made quite an impression on some whites. For those partial to the revolutionary movement especially, it became harder and harder to reconcile American claims to natural-born rights with the system of slavery. In this part of his original draft of the Declaration of Independence, Thomas Jefferson blamed slavery on King George III. But while they were willing to agree that the king should be held to account for what seemed like a British conspiracy against American liberties, other members of the Continental Congress did not approve of the explicit criticism of slavery expressed by Jefferson. If it had been adopted as written by Jefferson, the Declaration of Independence would have committed the American republic to ending slavery. Instead, the declaration adopted by the Second Continental Congress on July 4, 1776, mentions slavery only to blame the British forces for inciting slaves, like Indians, to fight against the colonists.**

WHEREAS the NEGROES in the counties of Briſtol and Worceſter, the 24th of March laſt, petitioned the Committees of Correſpondence for the county of Worceſter (then convened in Worceſter) to aſſiſt them in obtaining their freedom. **THEREFORE,**
In County Convention, June 14th, 1775.
RESOLVED, That we abhor the enſlaving of any of the human race, and particularly of the NEGROES in this country. And that whenever there ſhall be a door opened, or opportunity preſent, for any thing to be done toward the emancipating the NEGROES; we will uſe our influence and endeavour that ſuch a thing may be effected, *Atteſt.* WILLIAM HENSHAW, Clerk.

*The Massachusetts Spy, a Patriot paper whose masthead included the slogan "Undaunted by Tyrants we'll Die or be Free," ran this notice from the Worcester County Convention declaring the committee's resolve to influence the emancipation of the slaves. For some Patriots, the promise of "liberty for all" did not end with white men.*

He [the King] has waged cruel war against human nature itself, violating it's most sacred rights of life & liberty in the persons of a distant people, who never offended him captivating and carrying them into slavery in another hemisphere or to incur miserable death in their transportation thither. This piratical warfare, the opprobrium of *infidel* powers, is the warfare of the *Christian* king of Great Britain. Determined to keep open a market where MEN should be bought & sold, he has prostituted his negative for suppressing every legislative attempt to prohibit or to restrain this execrable commerce. And that this assemblage of horrors might want no fact of distinguished die, he in now exciting those very people to rise in arms among us, and to purchase that liberty of which *he* has deprived them, by murdering the people upon whom *he* also obtruded them: thus paying off former crimes committed against the *liberties* of one *people*, with crimes which he urges them to commit against the *lives* of another.

**Whether or not it dealt with slavery, the Declaration of Independence officially committed those who supported the Revolution to the principle of liberty. Soon after the document was published in July 1776, Lemuel Haynes, a free mulatto, a former Minuteman in his hometown of Granville, Massachusetts, and by October of that year a private in the Continental army, wrote an essay entitled "Liberty Further Extended; or, Free Thoughts on the Illegality of Slave-keeping." He began with a quote from the Declaration of Independence: "We hold these truths to be self-Evident, that all men are created Equal, that they are Endowed by their Creator with [Certain] unalienable rights, and among these**

*Reverend Lemuel Haynes spoke out against slavery from the pulpit after fighting for the Patriots in the Revolutionary War. He served several congregations in his native New England before his death in 1833, and his 1805 sermon "Universal Salvation" was widely published.*

are Life, Liberty, and the pursuit of happyness." Eventually, Haynes became a well-known minister who preached to white and black congregations in New England.

Haynes's essay, or sermon, is important as another example of black revolutionary antislavery protest. It takes the earlier petitions a step further, in keeping with the changing situation of 1776. If America was now a nation, what kind of a nation would it be? If liberty was natural, why should it belong only to white Americans of English descent and not to Africans?

But I query, whether Liberty is so contracted a principle as to be Confin'd to any nation under Heaven; nay, I think it not hyperbolical to affirm, that Even an affrican, has Equally as good a right to his Liberty in common with Englishmen.

I know that those that are concerned in the Slave-trade, Do pretend to Bring arguments in vindication of their practise; yet if we give them a candid Examination, we shall find them (Even those of the most cogent kind) to be Essencially Deficent. We live in a day wherein *Liberty & freedom* is the subject of many millions Concern; and the important Struggle hath alread caused great Effusion of Blood; men seen to manifest the most sanguine resolution not to Let their natural rights go without their Lives go with them; a resolution, one would think Every one that has the Least Love to his country, or futer posterity, would fully confide in, yet while we are so zelous to maintain, and foster our own invaded rights, it cannot be tho't impertinent for us Candidly to reflect on our own conduct, and I doubt not But that we shall find that subsisting in the midst of us, that may with propriety be stiled *Opression*, nay, much great oppression, than that which Englishmen seem so much to spurn at. I mean an oppression which they themselves, impose upon others. . . .

It hath pleased god to *make of one Blood all nations of men, for to dwell upon the face of the Earth.* Acts 17, 26. And as all are of one Species, so there are the same Laws, and aspiring principles placed in all nations; and the Effect that these Laws will produce, are Similar to Each other. Consequently we may suppose, that what is precious to one man, is precious to another, and what is irksom, or intolarable to one man, is so to another, consider'd in a Law of Nature. Therefore we may reasonably Conclude, that Liberty is Equally as pre[c]ious to a *Black man*, as it is to a *white one*, and Bondage Equally as intollarable to the one as it is to the other: Seeing it Effects the Laws of nature Equally as much in the one as it Does in the other.

But, as I observed Before, those privileges that are granted to us By the Divine Being, no one has the Least right to take them from us without our consen[t]; and there is Not the Least precept, or practise, in the Sacred Scriptures, that constitutes a Black man a Slave, any more than a white one.

# Revolutionary Soldiers

**For some slaves, as Lemuel Haynes probably thought, the best chance for further freedom lay with the Patriots; for others, it lay in fighting against the Patriots. In his _Narrative of Some of the Adventures, Dangers and Sufferings of a Revolutionary Soldier_ (1830), Private Joseph Plumb Martin remembered one slave who found Loyalism more useful than the Declaration of Independence. Although Martin makes fun of this African American as "a great politician," and insists that this slave must have received his Tory ideas from his master, the master certainly did not want his slave to take his Loyalism so seriously as to run away to join the British army. The independence of mind displayed by this slave and his ability to use the fight between whites to his advantage seem to have disturbed Private Martin as much as they angered the slave owner. Both preferred to think of Cuff finally "laid on his back" rather than talking back or fleeing.**

The man of the house where I was quartered had a smart-looking Negro man, a great politician. I chanced one day to go into the barn where he was threshing. He quickly began to upbraid me with my opposition to the British. The King of England was a very powerful prince, he said, a very powerful prince, and it was a pity that the colonists had fallen out with him; but as we had, we must abide by the consequences. I had no inclination to waste the shafts of my rhetoric upon a Negro slave. I concluded that he had heard his betters say so. As the old cock crows, so crows the young one, and I thought as the white cock crows, so crows the black one. He ran away from his master before I left there and went to Long Island to assist King George. But it seems the King of Terrors was more potent than King George, for his master had certain intelligence that Poor Cuff was laid flat on his back.

**The events of the Revolutionary War led to many dangers and abrupt changes for American slaves. In his _Memoirs of the Life of Boston King, a Black Preacher, Written by Himself,_**

## A Melancholy Impression

*John Adams, a Patriot leader from Massachusetts and a member of the Continental Congress, spoke with some of the delegates from the southern colonies and recorded his impressions in his diary.*

These gentlemen gave a melancholy impression of the State of Georgia and South Carolina. They say that if one thousand regular troops should land in Georgia, and their commander is provided with arms and clothes enough, and proclaim to all the negroes, who would join his camp, twenty thousand negroes would join it from the two Provinces in a fortnight. The negroes have a wonderful art of communicating intelligence among themselves; it will run several hundred miles in a week or fortnight. They say, their only security is this; that all the king's friends, and tools of government, have large plantations, and property in negroes; so that the slaves of the Tories would be lost, as well as those of the Whigs.

*during His Residence at Kingswood-School,* **published in the English** *Methodist Magazine* **(March 1798), King remembered that his first taste of "liberty" came after he ran away to the British troops stationed at Charleston, South Carolina, rather than face his angry master. During the war he remained in service, and only luck—and illness—prevented his recapture. But he exercised more and more control over his fate. For King, the war created conditions for freedom even as it led to danger and uncertainty. After the British evacuated New York in 1783, he went to Nova Scotia with 3,000 other black Loyalists.**

When 16 years old, I was bound apprentice to a trade. After being in the shop about two years, I had the charge of my master's tools, which being very good, were often used by the men, if I happened to be out of the way: When this was the case, or any of them were lost, or misplaced, my master beat me severely, striking me upon the head, or any other part with out mercy. One time in the holy-days, my master and the men being from home, and the care of the house devolving upon me and the younger apprentices, the house was broke open, and robbed of many valuable articles, thro' the negligence of the apprentice who had then the charge of it. When I came home in the evening, and saw what had happened, my consternation was inconceivable, as all that we had in the world could not make good the loss. The week following, when the master came to town, I was beat in a most unmerciful manner, so that I was not able to do any thing for a fortnight.

About eight months after, we were employed in building a store-house, and nails were very dear at that time, it being the American war, so that the work-men had their nails weighed out to them; on this account they made the younger apprentices watch the nails while they were at dinner. It being my lot one day to take care of them, which I did till an apprentice returned to his work, and then I went to dine. In the mean time he took away all the nails belonging to one of the journeymen, and he being of a very violent temper, accused me to the master with stealing of them. For this offence I was beat and tortured most cruelly, and was laid up three weeks before I was able to do any work. My proprietor, hearing of the bad usage I received, came to town, and severely reprimanded my master for beating me in such a manner, threatening him, that if he ever heard the like again, he would take me away and put me to another master to finish my time, and make him pay for it. This had a good effect, and he behaved much better to me, the two succeeding years, and I began to acquire a proper knowledge of my trade.

My master being apprehensive that Charles-Town was in danger on account of the war, removed into the country, about 38 miles off. Here we built a large house for Mr. Waters, during which time the English took Charles-Town. Having obtained leave one day to see my parents, who lived about 12 miles off, and it being late before I could go, I was obliged to borrow one of Mr. Water's horses; but a servant of my master's, took the horse from me to go a little journey, and stayed two or three days longer than he ought. This involved me in the greatest perplexity, and I expected the severest punishment, because the gentleman to whom the horse belonged was a very bad man, and knew not how to shew mercy. To escape his cruelty, I determined to go to Charles-Town, and throw myself into the hands of the English. They received me readily, and I began to feel the happiness of liberty, of which I knew nothing before, altho' I was much grieved at first, to be obliged to leave my friends, and reside among strangers. In this situation I was seized with the small-pox, and suffered great hardships; for all the Blacks affected with the disease, were ordered to be carried a mile from the camp, lest the soldiers should be infected, and disabled from marching. This was a grievous circumstance to me and many others. We lay sometimes a whole day without any thing to eat or drink; but Providence sent a man, who belonged to the York volunteers whom I was acquainted with, to my relief. He brought me such things as I stood in need of; and by the blessing of the Lord I began to recover.

By this time, the English left the place; but as I was unable to march with the army, I expected to be taken by the enemy. However when they came, and understood that we were ill of the small-pox, they precipitately left us for fear of the infection. Two days after, the waggons were sent to convey us to the English Army, and we were put into a little cottage, (being 25 in number) about a quarter of a mile from the Hospital.

Being recovered, I marched with the army to Chamblem. When we came to the head-quarters, our regiment was 35 miles

NEW-YORK, 21ˢᵗ April 1783.

THIS is to certify to whomsoever it may concern, that the Bearer hereof Cato Ramsay a Negro, resorted to the British Lines, in consequence of the Proclamations of Sir William Howe, and Sir Henry Clinton, late Commanders in Chief in America; and that the said Negro has hereby his Excellency Sir Guy Carleton's Permission to go to Nova-Scotia, or wherever else He may think proper.

By Order of Brigadier General Birch,

This pass was issued to a black soldier who served the Loyalist forces, granting him permission to emigrate to Nova Scotia. At the close of the war, the British and Americans had to decide the fate of the newly freed black Loyalist soldiers, and emigration was one way to resolve their ambiguous status.

*The instability caused by the Revolutionary War offered slaves an opportunity to escape their masters. Titus, whose owner advertised for his return, used the opportunity to join the British forces. He later gained fame as Captain Tye while fighting rebels in Monmouth County, New Jersey.*

> **THREE POUNDS Reward.**
>
> RUN away from the fubfcriber, living in Shrewfbury, in the county of Monmouth, New-Jerfey, a NEGROE man, named TITUS, but may probably change his name; he is about 21 years of age, not very black, near 6 feet high; had on a grey homefpun coat, brown breeches, blue and white ftockings, and took with him a wallet, drawn up at one end with a ftring, in which was a quantity of clothes. Whoever takes up faid Negroe, and fecures him in any goal, or brings him to me, fhall be entitled to the above reward of *Three Pounds* proc. and all reafonable charges, paid by
>
> *Nov. 8, 1775.* § JOHN CORLIS.

off. I stayed at the head-quarters three weeks, during which time our regiment had an engagement with the Americans, and the man who relieved me when I was ill of the small-pox, was wounded in the battle, and brought to the hospital. As soon as I heard of his misfortune, I went to see him, and tarried with him in the hospital six weeks, till he recovered; rejoicing that it was in my power to return him the kindness he had shewed me. . . . I tarried with Captain Grey about a year, and then left him, and came to Nelson's ferry. Here I entered into the service of the commanding officer of that place. But our situation was very precarious, and we expected to be made prisoners every day; for the Americans had 1600 men, not far off; whereas our whole number amounted only to 250; But there were 1200 English about 30 miles off; only we knew not how to inform them of our danger, as the Americans were in possession of the country. Our commander at length determined to send me with a letter, promising me great rewards, if I was successful in the business. I refused going on horse-back, and set off on foot about 3 o'clock in the afternoon; I expected every morning to fall in with the enemy, whom I well knew would shew me no mercy. I went on without interruption, till I got within six miles of my journey's end, and then was alarmed with a great noise a little before me. But I stepped out of the road, and fell flat upon my face till they were gone by. I then arose, and praised the Name of the Lord for his great mercy, and again pursued my journey, till I came to Mums-corner tavern. I knocked at the door, but they blew out the candle. I knocked again, and intreated the master to open the door. At last he came with a frightful countenance, and said, "I thought it was the Americans; for they were here about an hour ago, and I thought they were returned again." I asked, How many were there? he answered, "about one hundred." I desired him to saddle his horse for me, which he did, and went with me himself. When we had gone about two miles, we were stopped by the picket-guard, till the Captain came out with 30 men: As soon as he knew that I had brought an express from Nelson's-ferry, he received me with great kindness, and expressed his approbation of my courage and conduct in this dangerous business. Next morning, Colonel Small gave me three shillings, and many fine promises, which were all that I ever received for this service from him. However he sent 600 men to relieve the troops at Nelson's-ferry.

Soon after I went to Charles-Town, and entered on board a man of war. As we were going to Chesepeak-bay, we were at the taking of a rich prize. We stayed in the bay two days, and then sailed for New-York, where I went on shore. Here I endeavoured to follow my trade, but for want of tools was obliged to relinquish it, and enter into service. But the wages were so low that I was not able to keep myself in clothes, so that I was under the necessity of leaving my master and going to another. I stayed with him four months, but he never paid me, and I was obliged to leave him also, and work about the town until I was married. . . . Notwithstanding which, my mind was sorely distressed at the thought of being again reduced to slavery, and separated from my wife and family; and at the same time it was exceeding difficult to escape from my bondage, because the river at Amboy was above a mile over, and likewise another to cross at Staten-Island. I called to remembrance the many great deliverances the Lord had wrought for me, and besought him to save me this once, and I would serve him all the days of my life. While my mind was thus exercised, I went into the jail to see a lad whom I was acquainted with at New-York. He had been taken prisoner, and attempted to make his escape, but was caught 12 miles off: They tied him to the tail of a horse, and in this manner brought him back to Brunswick. When I saw him, his feet were fastened in the stocks, and at night both his hands. This was a terrifying sight to me, as I expected to meet with the same kind of treatment, if taken in the act of attempting to regain my liberty. I was thankful that I was not confined in a jail, and my master used me as well as I could expect; and indeed the slaves about Baltimore, Philadelphia, and New-York, have as good victuals as many of the English; for they have meat once a day, and milk for breakfast and supper; and what is better than all, many of the master send their slaves to school at night, that they may learn to read the Scriptures. This is a privilege indeed. But alas, all these enjoyments

*Lord Dunmore's proclamation did not go unanswered. The Virginia General Convention declared that slaves who "conspir[ed] to rebel" would be put to death, but those who surrendered to the Continental army would be pardoned.*

By the **REPRESENTATIVES** *of the* **PEOPLE** *of the Colony and Dominion of* VIRGINIA, *assembled in* GENERAL CONVENTION.

# A DECLARATION.

WHEREAS lord Dunmore, by his proclamation, dated on board the ship William, off Norfolk, the 7th day of November 1775, hath offered freedom to such able-bodied flaves as are willing to join him, and take up arms, against the good people of this colony, giving thereby encouragement to a general insurrection, which may induce a necessity of inflicting the severest punishments upon those unhappy people, already deluded by his base and insidious arts; and whereas, by an act of the General Assembly now in force in this colony, it is enacted, that all negro or other flaves, conspiring to rebel or make insurrection, shall suffer death, and be excluded all benefit of clergy: We think it proper to declare, that all flaves who have been, or shall be seduced, by his lordship's proclamation, or other arts, to desert their masters' service, and take up arms against the inhabitants of this colony, shall be liable to such punishment as shall hereafter be directed by the General Convention. And to the end that all such, who have taken this unlawful and wicked step, may return in safety to their duty, and escape the punishment due to their crimes, we hereby promise pardon to them, they surrendering themselves to col. William Woodford, or any other commander of our troops, and not appearing in arms after the publication hereof. And we do farther earnestly recommend it to all humane and benevolent persons in this colony to explain and make known this our offer of mercy to those unfortunate people. EDMUND PENDLETON, president.

could not satisfy me without liberty! Sometimes I thought, if it was the will of God that I should be a slave, I was ready to resign myself to his will; but at other times I could not find the least desire to content myself in slavery.

Being permitted to walk about when my work was done, I used to go to the ferry, and observed, that when it was low water the people waded across the river; tho' at the same time I saw there were guards posted at the place to prevent the escape of prisoners and slaves. As I was at prayer one Sunday evening, I thought the Lord heard me and would mercifully deliver me. Therefore putting my confidence in him, about one o'clock in the morning I went down to the river side, and found the guards were either asleep or in the tavern. I instantly entered into the river, but when I was a little distance from the opposite shore, I heard the sentinels disputing among themselves: One said, "I am sure I saw a man cross the river." Another replied, "There is no such thing." It seems they were afraid to fire at me, or make an alarm, lest they should be punished for their negligence. When I had got a little distance from the shore, I fell down upon my knees, and thanked God for this deliverance. I travelled till about five in the morning, and then concealed myself till seven o'clock at night, when I proceeded forward, thro' bushes and marshes, near the road, for fear of being discovered. When I came to the river, opposite Staten-Island, I found a boat; and altho' it was very near a whale-boat, yet I ventured into it, and cutting the rope, got safe over. The commanding officer, when informed of my case, gave me a passport, and I proceeded to New-York.

**The small state of Rhode Island filled out its two Continental army regiments with several hundred slaves and free blacks. More than 50 years later, Jehu Grant, one of those soldiers, wrote to the commissioner of pensions. The government did not approve his pension when he applied in 1832, for the reason that he had run away from his master: government officials were very sensitive to the issue of runaways in the 1830s because of southern masters' anger about abolitionism. Grant maintained that he believed in the Revolutionary cause and that his master had been a secret Tory, so that in running away he had served the cause as well as his own desire to be free.**

That he was a slave to Elihu Champlen who resided at Narraganset, Rhode Island. At the time he left him his said master was called a Tory and in a secret manner furnished the enemy when shipping lay nearby with sheep, cattle, cheese, etc., and received goods from them. And this applicant being afraid his said master would send him to the British ships, ran away sometime in August 1777, as near as he can recollect, being the same summer that Danbury was burnt. That he went right to Danbury after he left his said master and enlisted to Capt[ain] Giles Galer for eighteen months. That, according to the best of his memory, General Huntington and General Meigs's brigades, or a part of them, were at that place. That he, the applicant, was put to teaming with a team of horses and wagon, drawing provisions and various other loading for the army for three or four months until winter set in, then was taken as a servant to John Skidmore, wagon master general (as he was called), and served with him as his waiter until spring, when the said troops went to the Highlands or near that place on the Hudson River, a little above the British lines. That this applicant had charge of the team as wagoner and carried the said General Skidmore's baggage and continued with him and the said troops as his wagoner near the said lines until sometime in June, when his said master either sent or came, and this applicant was given up to his master again, and he returned, after having served nine or ten months.

**In 1836, Jehu Grant wrote another letter to the commissioner of pensions to corroborate this testimony.**

I was then grown to manhood, in the full vigor and strength of life, and heard much about the cruel and arbitrary things done by the British. Their ships lay within a few miles of my master's house, which stood near the shore, and I was confident that my master traded with them, and I suffered much from fear that I should be sent aboard a ship of war. This I disliked. But when I saw liberty poles and the people all engaged for the support of freedom, I could not but like and be pleased with such thing (God forgive me if I sinned in so feeling). And living on the borders of Rhode Island, where whole companies of colored people enlisted, it added to my fears and dread of being sold to the British. These considerations induced me to enlist into the American army,

*This document certifies that Beriah Bill, a resident of Norwich, Connecticut, enlisted "a Negro man named Barkus . . . into the Continental Service During The War. . . after [he] had Purchased him." Barkus Fox and other slaves served in the place of whites whose towns owed soldiers to the militia or the Continental army.*

where I served faithful about ten months, when my master found and took me home. Had I been taught to read or understand the precepts of the Gospel, "Servants obey your masters," I might have done otherwise, notwithstanding the songs of liberty that saluted my ear, thrilled through my heart. But feeling conscious that I have since compensated my master for the injury he sustained by my enlisting, and that God has forgiven me for so doing, and that I served my country faithfully, and that they having enjoyed the benefits of my service to an equal degree for the length [of] time I served with those generally who are receiving the liberalities of the government, I cannot but feel it becoming me to pray Your Honor to review my declaration on file and the papers herewith amended.

A few years after the war, Joshua Swan, Esq., of Stonington purchased me of my master and agreed that after I had served him a length of time named faithfully, I should be free. I served him to his satisfaction and so obtained my freedom. He moved into the town of Milton, where I now reside, about forty-eight years ago. After my time expired with Esq. Swan, I married a wife. We have raised six children. Five are still living. I must be upward of eighty years of age and have been blind for many years, and, notwithstanding the aid I received from the honest industry of my children, we are still very needy and in part are supported from the benevolence of our friends. With these statements and the testimony of my character herewith presented, I humbly set my claim upon the well-known liberality of the government.

*Most respectfully your humble servant*
     his
Jehu  x  Grant
    mark

# Equality Disputed

**By the Revolutionary era, an increasing number of whites in the colonies believed that slavery was an outmoded institution. In his *Notes on the State of Virginia* (1787), Thomas Jefferson related how a committee formed by the Virginia House of Burgesses had raised the possibility of gradually emancipating Virginia's slaves. But even though Jefferson wrote in the Declaration of Independence that "all men are created equal," and even though he criticized slavery as unjust in his original draft, he did not believe in African-American equality. In the *Notes* he again criticized slavery,**

but he also went to great lengths to justify his opposition to a free black presence in the new nation, proposing instead that liberated slaves be colonized in Africa. Because he was such an important revolutionary Patriot—he later served as secretary of state and as President of the United States—Jefferson's arguments against black equality were quite influential and became a target for both whites and blacks who wished to fight racism. Those who criticized Jefferson knew that these assertions of black inferiority helped ensure that free blacks, in the South and North, would not receive the same rights as whites in the new republic.

Virginia did not abolish slavery after the Revolution, but its citizens continued to debate the issue. Many of them acted on their own to free their slaves. As a result, the free black population of the southern and northern states continued to grow, which made slaveholders nervous and led to even more proposals to colonize the freed slaves outside the boundaries of the slave states.

*While many slaves ran away to join the Loyalist forces, others fought for the Patriot cause. This flag was presented to an all-black unit of Patriot soldiers, the "Bucks of America," by John Hancock at the end of the war as a tribute to their courage and dedication. However, most African Americans who fought for the Patriots served in integrated units.*

Many of the laws which were in force during the monarchy being relative merely to that form of government, or inculcating principles inconsistent with republicanism, the first assembly which met after the establishment of the commonwealth appointed a committee to revise the whole code. . . .The following are the most remarkable alterations proposed. . . .

To emancipate all slaves born after passing the act. The bill reported by the revisors does not itself contain this proposition; but an amendment containing it was prepared, to be offered the legislature whenever the bill should be taken up, and further directing, that they should continue with their parents to a certain age, then be brought up, at the public expence, to tillage, arts or sciences, according to their geniusses, till the females should be eighteen, and the males twenty-one years of age, when they should be colonized to such place as the circumstances of the time should render most proper, sending them out with arms, implements of household and of the handicraft arts, seeds, pairs of the useful domestic animals, &c. to declare them a free and independant people, and extend to them our alliance and protection, till they have acquired strength; and to send vessels to the other parts of the world for an equal number of white inhabitants; to induce whom to migrate hither, proper encouragements were to be proposed. It will probably be asked, Why not retain and incorporate the blacks into the state, and thus save the expence of supplying, by importation of white settlers, the vacancies they will leave? Deep rooted prejudices entertained by the whites; ten thousand recollections, by the blacks, of the injuries they have sustained; new provocations; the real distinctions which nature has made; and many other circumstances, will divide us into parties, and produce convulsions which will probably never end but in the extermination of one or the other race. . . .

Comparing them by their faculties of memory, reason, and imagination, it appears to me, that in memory they are equal to the whites; in reason much inferior, as I think one could scarcely be found capable of tracing and comprehending the investigations of Euclid; and that in imagination they are dull, tasteless, and anomalous. . . . Religion indeed has produced a Phyllis Wh[eat]ly; but it could not produce a poet. The compositions published under her name are below the dignity of criticism. . . . I advance it therefore as a suspicion only, that the blacks, whether originally a distinct race, or made distinct by time and circumstances, are inferior to the whites in the endowments of both body and mind.

**Jefferson's challenge to black abilities did not go unanswered. His argument for black inferiority rested on flimsy grounds—including the supposed lack of achievement of American slaves and free blacks. Benjamin Banneker (1731–1806), a free black who lived in Maryland, was a farmer with a passionate interest in mathematics and astronomy. In 1790 he performed the astronomical calculations for an almanac—a small annual book that helped colonial farmers by predicting the times of sunrise and sunset, the weather, tides, and other important information. When friends helped him publish the almanac (which, like Phillis Wheatley's poems, appeared with an engraved picture of its black author next to the title), he wasted no time in sending a copy to Jefferson, now U.S. secretary of state, with the following letter.**

*Maryland, Baltimore County, August 19, 1791.*
SIR,

I am fully sensible of the greatness of that freedom, which I take with you on the present occasion; a liberty which seemed to me scarcely allowable, when I reflected on that distinguished and dignified station in which you stand, and the almost general prejudice and prepossession, which is so prevalent in the world against those of my complexion.

I suppose it is a truth too well attested to you, to need a proof here, that we are a race of beings, who have long labored under the abuse and censure of the world; that we have long been looked upon with an eye of contempt; and that we have long been considered rather as brutish than human, and scarcely capable of mental endowments.

Sir, I hope I may safely admit, in consequence of that report which hath reached me, that you are a man far less inflexible in sentiments of this nature, than many others; that you are measurably friendly, and well disposed towards us; and that you are willing and ready to lend your aid and assistance to our relief, from those many distresses, and numerous calamities, to which we are reduced.

Now Sir, if this is founded in truth, I apprehend you will embrace every opportunity, to eradicate that train of absurd and false ideas and opinions, which so generally prevails with respect to us; and that your sentiments are concurrent with mine, which are, that one universal Father hath given being to us all; and that he hath not only made us all of one flesh, but that he hath also, without partiality, afforded us all the same sensations and endowed us all with the same faculties; and that however variable we may be in society or religion, however diversified in situation or color, we are all of the same family, and stand in the same relation to him.

Sir, if these are sentiments of which you are fully persuaded, I hope you cannot but acknowledge, that it is the indispensable duty of those, who maintain for themselves the rights of human nature, and who possess the obligations of Christianity, to extend their power and influence to the relief of every part of the human race, from whatever burden or oppression they may unjustly labor under; and this I apprehend, a full conviction of the truth and obligation of these principles should lead all to.

Sir, I have long been convinced, that if your love for yourselves, and for those inestimable laws, which preserved to you the rights of human nature, was founded on sincerity, you could not but be solicitous, that every individual, of whatever rank or distinction, might with you equally enjoy the blessings thereof; neither could you rest satisfied short of the most active effusion of your exertions, in order to their promotion from any state of degradation, to which the unjustifiable cruelty and barbarism of men may reduced them.

Sir, I freely and cheerfully acknowledge, that I am of the African race, and in that color which is natural to them of the

*Although Benjamin Banneker's name is misspelled on this title page, he believed that his almanac, the first scientific book published by an African American, would persuade Thomas Jefferson that blacks were not the intellectual inferiors of whites.*

*Thomas Jefferson's cordial reply to Benjamin Banneker acknowledges Banneker's accomplishment as a scientist and asserts his own desire to "rais[e] the condition" of blacks. However, his phrase "the imbecility of their present existence" indicates his persistent belief in the inferiority of blacks.*

deepest dye; and it is under a sense of the most profound gratitude to the Supreme Ruler of the Universe, that I now confess to you, that I am not under that state of tyrannical thraldom, and inhuman captivity, to which too many of my brethren are doomed, but that I have abundantly tasted of the fruition of those blessings, which proceed from that free and unequalled liberty with which you are favored; and which, I hope, you will willingly allow you have mercifully received from the immediate hand of that Being, from whom proceedeth every good and perfect Gift.

Sir, suffer me to recal to your mind that time, in which the arms and tyranny of the British crown were exerted, with every powerful effort, in order to reduce you to a state of servitude: look back, I entreat you, on the variety of dangers to which you were exposed; reflect on that time in which every human aid appeared unavailable, and in which even hope and fortitude wore the aspect of inability to the conflict, and you cannot but be led to a serious and grateful sense of your miraculous and providential preservation; you cannot but acknowledge, that the present freedom and tranquility which you enjoy you have mercifully received, and that it is the peculiar blessing of Heaven.

This, Sir, was a time when you clearly saw into the injustice of a state of slavery, and in which you had just apprehensions of the horrors of its condition. It was now that your abhorrence thereof was so excited, that you publicly held forth this true and invaluable doctrine, which is worthy to be recorded and remembered in all succeeding ages: "We hold these truths to be self-evident, that all men are created equal; that they are endowed by their Creator with certain unalienable rights, and that among these are, life, liberty, and the pursuit of happiness."

Here was a time, in which your tender feelings for yourselves had engaged you thus to declare, you were then impressed with proper ideas of the great violation of liberty, and the free possession of those blessings, to which you were entitled by nature; but, Sir, how pitiable is it to reflect, that although you were so fully convinced of the benevolence of the Father of Mankind, and of his equal and impartial distribution of these rights and privileges, which he hath conferred upon them, that you should at the same time counteract his mercies, in detaining by fraud and violence so numerous a part of my brethren, under groaning captivity and cruel oppression, that you should at the same time be found guilty of that most criminal act, which you professedly detested in others, with respect to yourselves.

I suppose that your knowledge of the situation of my brethren, is too extensive to need a recital here; neither shall I presume to prescribe methods by which they may be relieved, otherwise than by recommending to you and all others, to wean yourselves from those narrow prejudices which you have imbibed with respect to them, and as Job proposed to his friends, "put your soul in their souls' stead;" thus shall your hearts be enlarged with kindness and benevolence towards them; and thus shall you need neither the direction of myself or others, in what manner to proceed herein.

And now, Sir, although my sympathy and affection for my brethren hath caused my enlargement thus far, I ardently hope, that your candor and generosity will plead with you in my behalf, when I make known to you, that it was not originally my design; but having taken up my pen in order to direct to you, as a present, a copy of an Almanac, which I have calculated for the succeeding year, I was unexpectedly and unavoidably led thereto.

This calculation is the production of my arduous study, in this my advanced stage of life; for having long had unbounded desires to become acquainted with the secrets of nature, I have had to gratify my curiosity herein, through my own assiduous application to Astronomical Study, in which I need not recount to you the many difficulties and disadvantages, which I have had to encounter.

And although I had almost declined to make my calculation for the ensuing year, in consequence of that time which I allotted therefor, being taken up at the Federal Territory, by the request of Mr. Andrew Ellicott, yet finding myself under several engagements to Printers of this state, to whom I had communicated my design, on my return to my place of residence, I industriously applied myself thereto, which I hope I have accomplished with correctness and accuracy; a copy of which I have taken the liberty to direct to you, and which I humbly request you will favorably receive; and although you may have the opportunity of perusing it after its

Mr. Andrew Ellicott . . . was employed by the President of the United States of America, to lay off the land, ten miles square, on the Potowmack, for the use of Congress. . . . He is attended by *Benjamin Banneker*, an Ethiopian, whose abilities as a surveyor, and an astronomer, clearly prove that Mr. Jefferson's concluding that race of men void of racial endowments, was without foundation.

—Georgetown *Weekly Ledger*, March 1791

publication, yet I choose to send it to you in manuscript previous thereto, that thereby you might not only have an earlier inspection, but that you might also view it in my own hand writing.

# Revolutionary Ideals

**African Americans considered their service in the Revolution to be a good reason to be granted their freedom, whether it was promised or not. In this petition to the assembly of the state of Connecticut, a group of slaves demanded, however humbly, freedom for all slaves in the state. They draw on the contemporary law of nations, which determined treatment of foreign nationals, to say that there is no place in law or right for their "Countrymen" to be held in bondage. Just as the Revolution gave Americans a sense of nationhood, so did African Americans begin to speak of themselves as one nation—a nation within a nation.**

To the Hon[ora]ble General assembly of the Governor & Company of the State of Connecticut sitting at new Haven this 2d Thursday of Oct. 1783

The Memorial of Charles Cato Frank Jack Cuff Yarrow & Abel Negroes & Servants for themselves and the rest of the Negro Servants in the State of Connecticut humbly sheweth

That Your Petitioners are now deemed & treated as Slaves the absolute Property of their masters altho. they never committed any Crime for which they ought to forfeit their Liberties or be deprived of their natural Right to Freedom. They would humbly suggest to your Honor whether they ought to be holden in Bondage merely on account of their Birth being born of black parents if this circumstance alone be sufficient entail slavery upon them & their offspring to all generations—and as they at first became the Pretended Property of their Masters from the Circumstances of their Ancestors having been perfidiously stolen from their Native Country and after being held by Force under the Power of those who then got them into Possession We their descendants have thereby become slaves being born of such parents and as the Indians their predecessors in Slavery were by the Justice of A great Monarch upon the incessant Applications of a great Friend to the rights of humankind freed from slavery & the negroes immediately brought into Bondage to supply their place have they not served their full term of servitude & if it is absolutely necessary that Slavery should exist ought not the Americans now to free the Negroes who have served so long a term & put some other Nation in their Place. this they think would be but justice to them however Colour may be denominated a proper criterion by which to Judge who ought be freed who in Slavery if the deformity of Body be deemed evidence of the want of rational faculties—And as many of them have had assurances from their Masters that if they would faithfully serve them during the War that they should be emancipated Yet those engagements are now forgot & they continued slaves tho their brethren who have served in arms are freed. They therefore pray, your Honour to Take their care into Your Serious consideration & grant them relief & freedom and as in Duty bound shall ever pray

 Cato, Frank, Jack, Cuff

 Yarrow & Abel for themselves

 and their Countrymen that are Slaves

**African Americans, slave and free, did not soon forget the promises of the Revolution. Nor did whites forget how revolutionary ideals, as much as wartime disorder, undermined slavery. In 1800, the slaves who participated in Gabriel's Rebellion in Virginia pursued these ideals, as the British traveler Robert Sutcliff reported in his *Travels in Some Parts of North America in the Years 1804, 1805, & 1806*.**

*9th Month, 25th.* I pursued my way to Richmond in the mail stage, through a beautiful country, but clouded and debased by Negro slavery. At the house where I breakfasted, which is called the Bowling-green, I was told that the owner had in his possession 200 slaves. In one field near the house, planted with tobacco, I counted nearly 20 women and children, employed in picking grubs from the plant. In the afternoon I passed by a field in which several poor slaves had lately been executed, on the charge of having an intention to rise against their masters. A lawyer who was present at their trials at Richmond, informed me that on one of them being asked, what he had to say to the court in his defence, he replied, in a manly tone of voice: "I have nothing more to offer than what General Washington would have had to offer, had he been taken by the British and put to trial by them. I have adventured my life in endeavoring to obtain the liberty of my countrymen, and am a willing sacrifice in their cause: and I beg, as a favour, that I may be immediately led to execution. I know that you have pre-determined to shed my blood, why then all this mockery of a trial?"

*Chapter Three*

# Forging Freedom and Fighting Slavery in the North

T he slave system came under attack as never before during the era of the American Revolution, especially in the northern colonies. Yet slavery in the North did not end with that war but continued in most of the northern states for decades afterward. Even those states that abolished slavery, such as Pennsylvania in 1780 and Connecticut in 1784, freed only those slaves who were born after certain dates. (The others were freed much later.) In 1799, New York enacted emancipation for all children of slaves born after the passage of the law but did not officially free every black until 1827. There were still slaves in rural New Jersey in the 1840s, and freed slaves throughout the North were often left without any property or means of support. As a result, young and old African Americans, born free or slave, often became indentured servants, or they became dependent on their former masters and mistresses. Thus the first emancipations in the United States are rightly called gradual. African Americans in the North continued to do the hardest work for the least pay and security.

The gradual liberation of slaves in the North was accompanied by other significant social changes: one of the greatest was a surge in the urban black population. Free blacks flocked to the cities in search of work, and freedom. For the first time in the North, African Americans found themselves able to project a unified voice on political

*Banners such as this were often hung at the large abolitionist meetings that took place in the North. By using the Liberty Bell, which was rung to announce American independence in 1776, abolitionists made a symbol of the American Revolution their own. For abolitionists, the struggle against slavery was a logical extension of the American Revolution.*

and social issues. They began to cooperate with white antislavery activists. At the same time, the complicated politics of slavery and emancipation led them to disagree with some of their white allies, and among themselves. The result was a distinctly modern form of African-American politics and activism. Black leaders emerged—and competed with each other—to speak for black America, to white America.

With the gradual liberation of northern slaves, the opposition to the continuation of slavery elsewhere in the nation gained ground among northern activists. The power of this growing anti-slavery opinion was limited, though, because of the further spread of slavery in the South. Thanks to westward expansion and a booming cotton economy, the South had become a wealthy region with reason and resources to expand slavery into new states such as Arkansas, Mississippi, and Texas. The simultaneous decline of slavery in the North and the growth of slavery in the South divided black and white northerners who were opposed to slavery into three groups. The first opposed slavery but believed that it would eventually die out as a system, as it seemed to have done in the North. Some of these people also considered them-selves part of a second group, the colonizationists—those who supported the idea of sending former slaves back to Africa to live in colonies and eventually establish themselves as citizens of new African nations. The third group—the smallest among whites but probably the largest among blacks—were abolitionists. They called for the immediate and total end of the institution of slavery, wherever it existed.

Although some northerners and whites of the Upper South (especially in Virginia and Kentucky) supported colonization, many blacks opposed the notion that they could be removed from American society. The memory of the Revolution and its ideals of liberty were still very much alive, and blacks recognized the huge contribution they had made to American independence as sol-diers, laborers, and spies. The continuation of racism and slavery, however, made some blacks and whites believe that people of African descent would have better chances at freedom in Africa.

Colonization remained a hot topic for the half century before the Civil War in part because it meant very different things to dif-ferent people. Proposals for colonization gained widespread support among whites because it allowed for the perpetuation of slavery without the necessity of accepting freed slaves into south-ern society. Colonization meant that freed blacks would be trans-ported to Africa, which would, in turn, free southerners from their mounting worries about slave revolts instigated by former slaves. But this justification caused many northerners who had supported colonization to turn to the cause of abolitionism. The southern view of colonization would, in reality, allow slavery to continue, and this truth contributed to the abolitionists' call for slavery's immediate end.

Despite the growing opposition to slavery, the roles played by black and white northerners in the antislavery struggle were by no means equal. As a result, the activism of northern free blacks came to be concerned with equality among the free in the North—that is, civil rights—as much as it was with the struggle on behalf of distant southern slaves. After the Revolution blacks began forming an organized identity separate from whites and created their own social institutions. Churches, in particular, became places where blacks could unite despite differences in education or class background. Such institutions were a crucial step in the formation of racial solidarity and identity, because the white abolitionist effort, like white society in general, often expected black individuals to work silently on behalf of an effort that they themselves did not direct. Yet it is doubtful that the abolitionist movement would have become a force for change without African Americans. By the 1830s, the movement was driving southern statesmen to invent new justifications for slavery, and abolitionists were upsetting the balance of power in the U.S. Congress between the slave and free states with their petitions against slavery and its expansion westward.

Many of the new black organizations in the North included the word *African* in their titles. These were purposeful efforts to create an identity different from the one implied by the racial term *black*. In an age when the people of the United States were proudly claiming a new national identity as Americans, people of African descent pointed out that they too were members of a nation—or a nation within a nation. But did this mean they were not really American, as some whites would claim? Or that they had two national identities? The discrimination to which blacks were subjected even while the antislavery movement gained strength—and gained the potential to upset the new American union—led their leaders to develop various, often conflicting, ways of talking about black community and identity. What did it mean to be a free black living in the North? What did it mean that blacks were still enslaved in the South? Where was the revolutionary notion of liberty, of "all men are created equal"? These questions were explored in numerous, quite public ways.

Abolitionism, in sum, was about more than slavery. Northern blacks simultaneously fought many battles around the question of race, as much in their private lives as over the public fate of their southern brothers and sisters. In this way, the first civil rights movement had its root in the struggle against slavery.

# First Steps to Freedom

**In 1808, a group of free blacks in Newport, Rhode Island, founded the African Benevolent Society. This society and other groups like it were organized responses to the growth of the northern free black community and its needs. Although it promoted racial pride and participation, the society's constitution reveals a larger political significance because it presumes African Americans acting as citizens in public life. The very word *constitution* in the title of this document calls to mind the U.S. Constitution, but the society's message was one of African autonomy and control of their own institutions. Although the African Benevolent Society's directors included whites, no vote was to be carried out without a majority of black directors present. In the larger world of American politics, by contrast, even free blacks in most states could not vote.**

*Constitution of the African Benevolent Society.*
INTRODUCTION.
WHEREAS the Sovereign Lord of the Universe, who *hath, of one blood, made all nations, to dwell on all the face of the earth,* hath been pleased, in various ways, to frown upon the African Nations, and hath placed us in circumstances of trial and depression;—we would humbly bow before him, and adore, his mysterious justice. At the same time, sensible of the great defects of school instruction amongst us, and of the numerous benefits which would result from securing the education of our children and friends after us,— Therefore,

1st. Resolved, That we form ourselves into a Society, to be called, the *African Benevolent Society;* and that our object shall be, the establishment and continuance of a free school, for any person of colour in this town.

Of MEMBERS.

2d. Any person of colour, whether male or female, may become a member of this Society, by subscribing to the Constitution, and by paying fifty Cents.

**Christian Sisters**

*Sarah L. Forten, daughter of James Forten, a black leader in Philadelphia, published this poem in the* Proceedings of the Anti-Slavery Convention *(1837).*

We are thy sisters. God has truly said,
That of one blood the nation he has made.
O, Christian woman! in a Christian land,
Canst thou unblushing read this great command?
Suffer the wrongs which wring our inmost heart,
To draw one throb of pity on thy part!
Our skins may differ, but from thee we claim
A sister's privilege and a sister's name.

3d. Any member residing in this place, and neglecting payment one year after it is due, shall be considered no longer a member of this Society. Any member may be dismissed, by expressing his desire to any three Directors; who shall see the word *Dismissed* written against his name.

Of OFFICERS.

4th. There shall be a President, Vice-President, a Secretary, Treasurer, and Eleven Directors.

5th. The President shall act as Moderator in the meetings of the Society; and, in his absence, the Vice-President shall act in his place.

6th. The Secretary shall record, in a book kept for that purpose, all the acts and doings of the Society; and shall write letters of Correspondence, &c. according to the direction and order of the Society, and shall have the care of the writings of the Society.

7. The Treasurer shall keep the money which shall belong to the Society; and shall keep a regular account of what he receives; and shall not pay any out, unless by order, or by application of the Directors; and shall exhibit a full statement to them, Quarterly, or yearly, as the Society shall direct.

8th. The Directors shall consist of four white and seven colored persons, who shall have no power, but in the capacity of Directors. The Directors shall have the complete management of the monies of the Society. They shall also provide the place for, and the Instructors of, the School; and shall determine what part of the year the School shall be opened. In short, they shall have the complete direction of the School; and shall render a full statement of their proceedings to the Society, at every Annual meeting; and they shall consult and unite, as far as they shall feel it a duty to promote the welfare of the Africans, with the Rhode-Island Missionary Society.

VOTES of the SOCIETY and DIRECTORS.

9th. Two thirds of the male members, residing in this place, shall be necessary to transact any business. In any questions before the Society, a Majority shall carry a Vote. The officers shall be elected orally or by ballot.

88 CHURCHES IN BOSTON.

**FIRST INDEPENDENT BAPTIST CHURCH,**

BELKNAP STREET.

This Church was constituted under the title of the 'African Baptist Church,' on the 5th day of August, A. D. 1805. It was incorporated under its present title, A. D. 1838.

PASTORS.

Rev. THOMAS PAUL, ind. 1805, dis. 1829.
Rev. WASHINGTON CHRISTIAN, ind. 1832, dis. 1832.
Rev. SAMUEL GOOCH, ind. 1832, dis. 1834.
Rev. JOHN GIVEN, ind. 1834, dis. 1835.
Rev. ARMSTRONG ARCHER, ind. 1836, dis. 1837.
Rev. GEORGE H. BLACK, ind. 1838, dis. 1841.
Rev. J. T. RAYMOND, ind. 1842, present Pastor.

Present number of members, 158.

The building, which was built by subscription, is situated in a court near Belknap street, adjoining the 'Smith School' edifice. It is very plain and commodious, being capable of seating 600 persons. The proprietors have it in contemplation, if the necessary means can be raised, to modernize, and otherwise improve the premises.

*For northern blacks, their churches served as centers of the community and as places to meet and discuss antislavery and civil rights issues. In the same spirit shared by many 19th-century black organizations, the First Independent Baptist Church in Boston was later named the African Meeting House to emphasize the congregation's African heritage.*

*Black and white abolitionists collaborated to create schools for freed people's children. Many of the free black leaders of the mid-19th century, such as Henry Highland Garnet and Alexander Crummell, studied at these schools.*

**NEW-YORK AFRICAN FREE-SCHOOL, No. 2.**
Engraved from a drawing taken by P. Reason, a pupil, aged 13 years.

10th. Seven of the Directors shall be the least number to transact business; and of the seven, two shall be white. Also no Vote shall be carried by the Directors, without the concurrence of a majority of the coloured, and at least Two of the white Directors.

Of the SCHOOL.

11th. The Instructor shall be one who believes in the duty of Prayer, and conscientiously conforms to it: and he shall cause the Scriptures to be read in School, daily.

He shall, also, pay special attention to the morals of the Scholars; and shall have power to enquire into their conduct out of School: and the School shall be visited, quarterly, by the Directors, who shall examine into the conduct and progress of the Scholars.

Of MEETINGS.

12th. The Society shall open and close their meetings with prayer. They shall meet annually, on the first Wednesday in January, for the purpose of paying their tax, of choosing officers, and of making arrangements for a public meeting, annually, on the second Thursday of April. At this meeting the Society shall elect, orally, or by ballot, some Minister of this place, to deliver a Discourse: or may agree to meet with the *Friends*, if they appoint a Meeting for them, on the said second Thursday of April: at which time the Friends of their Society shall be publicly invited, through

It is a well known fact, that black people, upon certain days of publick jubilee, dare not be seen after twelve o'clock in the day, upon the field to enjoy the times; for no sooner do the fumes of that potent devil, Liquor, mount into the brain, than the poor black is assailed like the destroying Hyena or the avaricious Wolf! I allude particularly to the FOURTH OF JULY!—Is it not wonderful, that the day set apart for the festival of Liberty, should be abused by the advocates of Freedom, in endeavoring to sully what they profess to adore.

—James Forten, *Letters from a Man of Colour on a Late Bill Before the Senate of Pennsylvania* (1813)

the medium of the News-paper, to attend, and to aid their object by a collection.—Also at this meeting a general statement of their circumstances shall be publicly made.

Of amending the CONSTITUTION.

13th. Any laws may be added by the Society; but the Articles concerning the manner of elections, and concerning the number of persons and power of the Directors, shall never be varied.

**In 1820, the *Carolina Centinel* of New Bern, North Carolina, reprinted a report of a near riot that occurred in Boston after a black man was arrested for the purpose of being shipped south to his alleged master. Such incidents took place regularly in northern cities. The *Boston Daily Advertiser*'s commentary below reveals whites' growing fear of organized groups of freed blacks. Despite increasing northern emancipation, the reality of southern slavery always remained a central concern for black northerners. Their actions alarmed many white Americans, northern and southern.**

*This poster announcing the kidnapping of the fugitive slave Anthony Burns in Boston reveals the powerful emotions the Fugitive Slave Bill aroused among abolitionists. The bill brought slavery to the North as it obligated northerners to assist in the capture of fugitive slaves. This vivid clash between the North and South proved to be a precursor to the Civil War.*

*Boston, Dec.* 30

### SERIOUS AFFRAY.

On Tuesday evening at near ten o'clock, a collection of between thirty & forty blacks, assembled for the purpose of liberating a black who had been imprisoned, and who it was understood by them was a slave, and was to be sent to one of the southern states to his master. The blacks were armed with bludgeons, & it was observed that they were stationed in couples at all the corners in Court street, and near the jail. They were observed by two young men returning to their lodgings, who suspecting their intentions were directed to no good purpose, gave information to the watchmen. One of the blacks was then heard to whistle, when he was immediately surrounded by upwards of twenty of his comrades. The watchmen on asking one of them what was their business was answered in a saucy manner; and soon after one of the blacks stepped from the side walk towards a watchman, who had his back to him, and knocked him down with his club. A number of the watchmen and citizens having now collected, attempted to secure all the blacks they could find, and succeeded in apprehending fifteen, who were all committed to jail.

Yesterday morning they were examined before Justice Gorham, on a charge of assaulting the watchmen, when four of them were committed for trial at the Municipal Court, on the first Monday in January next.

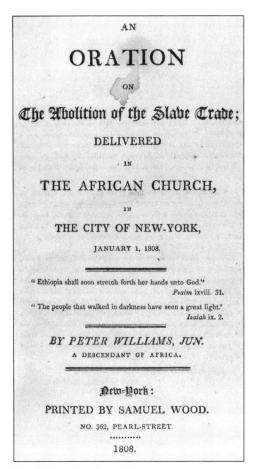

*The abolition of the slave trade was an important step toward ending slavery in the United States. The event was celebrated by the free black community in the North with speeches and marches.*

Mr. Fulton, the watchman who was knocked down, we understand is dangerously ill; and fears are entertained that he will not recover.

# An End to the Slave Trade

**The idealism voiced by Henry Sipkins in his speech on the first anniversary of the abolition of the American slave trade, which was ended in 1808, celebrates possibilities that later writers and speakers dismiss as fanciful. Sipkins does, however, raise concerns that develop over the following two decades into central themes of the black northern effort of racial uplift. Sipkins's criticisms of the slave trade from Africa to the Americas are also criticisms of slavery itself. Slavery is the source of degradation of Africans in Africa, in the British colonies, and in the United States. Its ending makes possible all kinds of progress, including the reunification of African princes and American slaves, perhaps through colonization.**

This day completes the first anniversary of the suspension of that facinerious [evil] traffic, which has made the most indelible blot in the history of nations. May it ever be held as a monument of contempt by rising generations. Rejoice that its baneful effects shall no longer be seen in these United States, nor the British colonies. No longer shall the shores of Africa be drenched with human gore. No longer shall its inhabitants be torn from their native soil; no longer shall they be brought on cruel shipboard, weighed down in chains; . . . nor shall the dismal groans of dying captives intercept our ears. No longer shall we witness the woeful prospect of an unnatural separation of a loving husband, an affectionate wife; nor a darling child cling to its fond parents, imploring their protection from the impending fury of their merciless owners. Rejoice, that no longer shall the sons of Africa become the subjects of such inhuman drudgery. Rejoice, my brethren, descendants of Africans, that the exiles of our race are emerging from the depths of forlorn slavery, in which they have been environed. The thick fogs of ignorance that have ever encompassed their gloomy mansions are gradually vanishing; they have been dissipated by the superior radiance of increasing knowledge. . . .

But may the long wished for time soon arrive when slavery of every species shall be destroyed—when despotism and oppression shall forever cease—when the Africans shall be reinstated in their former joys—when the exulting shouts of Princes, embracing their long lost oppressed subjects, shall reverberate on our ears—when the bursting acclamations of approbation shall resound from the tombs of our worthy departed ancestors; and all find protection under the fostering wing of Liberty.

**Great Britain abolished its slave trade in 1807 and the United States banned the American overseas slave trade after 1808, but what this meant for those already enslaved remained unclear. In Boston, New York, and Philadelphia, free blacks used the occasion to celebrate their own freedom and to argue for the abolition of all slavery. Every year, the anniversary of the passage of this national law created a white-sanctioned opportunity for black racial uplift, but it also rendered the African-American community vulnerable to white scrutiny. The following sympathetic report from the Boston newspaper *Columbian Centinel* on July 18, 1821, reveals that some whites did not cheer the parade. It also shows that blacks used the celebration, much as whites used the Fourth of July, to comment on the meaning of national events and local politics. The Massachusetts legislature had recently issued a report criticizing the free black community for its poverty and problems. The fourth toast responds, politely but firmly, to the unfair prejudices revealed in the report. Post-Revolutionary newspapers, which assumed that virtually all their readers were white, helped create such conflicting views of the activities of the black community and the significance of these happenings.**

## CELEBRATION OF FREEDOM

On Monday, the Africans, and descendants of Africans, in this town, held their annual commemoration of the commencement of measures for the abolition of the Slave Trade. A respectable Procession passed through many streets on the way to the African meeting-house. The Rev. HOSEA BALLOU delivered the discourse this year. A dinner was served up in the African school-house. The blessing was craved by the REV. THOMAS PAUL, and thanks returned by Mr. SAMUEL SNOWDEN. Every thing was conducted with decency and order, and the company returned to their homes two hours before sun setting. The streets were nearly as much thronged as they are on Election and

### The *Liberator*

*James Forten wrote to William Lloyd Garrison about Garrison's plan to establish a national antislavery newspaper in 1830.*

I am extremely happy to hear that you are about establishing a paper in Boston. I hope your efforts may not be in vain; and may the "Liberator" be the means of exposing, more and more, the odious system of Slavery, and of raising up friends to the oppressed and degraded People of Colour, throughout the Union.

*Antislavery women put on carnival fairs, where they sold goods they made or that had been donated. This ticket for admission suggests the purpose of the fair: to raise money for the cause. Some of the articles sold proclaimed an antislavery message, such as the quilt that serves as the frontispiece for this book.*

This broadside from about 1825 parodies the celebration of the abolition of the slave trade, mocks the dialect of free blacks, and lampoons the songs and toasts of these celebrations. As one of a series of broadsides, this parody reveals the discomfort these celebrations caused among whites.

Independent days, and as when President MONROE, and some of the Naval Worthies, passed there in procession; but the cheers were not so loud, nor so unanimous.

The following Toasts were given:—

*Wilberforce, Pitt[,] Fox, Clarkson, Greenville, Benezet, Woolman, Dickson, Marquis de la Fayette, Brissot, Claviere, Washington, Franklin, Adams, Jefferson, Madison, Monroe.* Names in the old and new world, which Africans and the descendants of Africans will long have reason to remember.

*The ever memorable vote for the Abolition of the Slave Trade in 1807, which was carried in the House of Lords in the affirmative, 100 to 16 and in the Commons 286 to 16.* The deed is registered in Heaven—The mandate is gone forth—Africa must and shall be free.

*Africa.*—She is free—when a nation of Africans can vindicate their claims to mental equality in the community of civilized man.

*The late report of the legislature of Massachusetts on the subject of "Free Blacks."* We wish the Gentlemen Committee a better acquaintance with us. For our characters, we refer to the merchants of Long, Central, and Indian wharves, and to those citizens, in whose families many of us have lived a great number of years, and from all whom we derive support for ourselves, our wives and our little ones.

**A second account of the same celebration of the abolition of the slave trade, from another Boston newspaper and reprinted in the Wilmington, Delware, *Christian Repository,* presents an unusually sympathetic view. It is clear here that blacks marching in the streets of Boston, protesting slavery and proclaiming their own freedom, met with a great deal of hostility.**

AFRICAN CELEBRATION.

In Boston, on July 16th, the *Sons of Africa* celebrated the anniversary of the abolition of the slave trade. A procession under the charge of marshals, and escorted by the African band of music, consisting of upwards of two hundred men, and followed by nearly one hundred boys, decorated with a rose, and the whole closed by thirty or forty old men, marched through some of the principal streets, to the African church, where a sermon was preached. We are willing to say that in this celebration our hearts rejoice. We are glad to see that day celebrated in which Wilberforce, Fox, Pitt, Grenville, Sharp, and a band of worthies conquered a nation and the world. Not indeed with the clash of swords and roar of cannon, and fields covered with carnage, but with bosoms glowing with philanthropy, with no other weapon but truth, hurled with resistless eloquence, they bore down a nation's prejudices, prostrated the falsehoods of interested men, and took the first triumphant step towards the freedom of a continent. We know that it is objected that the blacks are too degraded to undertake such a celebration. We ask, whose fault is this? and whose duty is it to raise them from this degradation? The poor Africans are shut out of society, out of employment, degraded by ourselves, and treated as cattle; and then we turn and demand that they should be wise and prudent and virtuous. And that they are not, we make a sufficient reason for further measures to degrade them. We are glad that there is one day in the year, in which the sons of Africa may know that they are men, and exercise something like national feeling. Another objection is, that this celebration presents inducements to the blacks to contract vices and spend their money. An objection which we acknowledge, and the weight of which we have often felt. We have only to say, that it lies no more against the holydays of black men, than of white men. Another is, that this parade produces a mob-like confusion, and the whole is turned into burlesque. We know the declaration is true, and we were sorry to see boys, whose parents ought to have taught them to respect the aged, of whatever color, preceding the procession on Monday, and treating its aged leaders in a manner which too well proves the deficiency of their education. We can at least say with respect to the good conduct of the blacks, that when white men chose to have a procession, they never make a mob. The fact is, that even in N[ew] England, our feelings towards black men need renovation. We must feel that they are our fellow beings, men as much as we, immortal men and many of them, at the bar of judgement, perhaps, to turn white by the side of those who now despise them. Their degradation must bring to our remembrance the wrongs they have suffered from white men, and instead of exciting our contempt, most excite our pity, and prompt us to make great efforts to enlighten and elevate their character.

## Opponents to Colonization

**In 1816, Paul Cuffe, a free black merchant and seaman, went to Africa and returned to promote colonization, and in that same year, the American Colonization Society was created. Soon afterward, however, black opposition to colonization began to be heard. Although the writers of the following resolutions from a public meeting held at an African church in**

### An Argument for Colonization

*Robert Goodloe Harper, a former U.S. senator from Maryland, was one of the first members of the American Colonization Society. His reasons for supporting colonization were very different from those of free blacks who were in favor of it. Harper's attitudes, in fact, help explain why most free blacks opposed colonization.*

It is not in themselves merely that the free people of color are a nuisance and burden. They contribute greatly to the corruption of the slaves, and to aggravate the evils of their condition, by rendering them idle, discontented, and disobedient.

*Though colonization was seen as a viable means of ending slavery by some blacks and whites, it was viewed by others as yet another white manipulation of blacks' lives. In this illustration from the 1839 Anti-Slavery Almanac, black men are being forced onto ships to return to Africa much as they were forced onto ships to come to America as slaves.*

Philadelphia do not declare themselves to be against colonization, they articulate this sentiment through the assertion of other inherent rights. Within the powerful social structure of the church, the voice of a black national identity began to form. Northern blacks were as concerned about the continuation of southern slavery as they were about their own disadvantaged position in the white community. The fact that whites were suggesting colonization for both northern and southern blacks—for the free and the slave—demanded a response that also considered the prospects of both groups to be one and inseparable.

James Forten and Russell Parrott, who led this meeting, gave orations on several anniversaries of the end of the slave trade. Parrott, a printer, had his speeches published and distributed them to sympathetic whites. This meeting was reported in a newspaper and the account was reprinted in William Garrison's *Thoughts on Colonization*.

## Discord in the Songs of Freedom

*The Reverend Peter Williams, Jr., of St. Philip's Church in New York City, was one of the first African Americans to give the kind of anti–July Fourth oration that Frederick Douglass perfected in 1852. This excerpt comes from* Williams's Discourse delivered in St. Philip's Church, for the benefit of the Coloured Community of Wilberforce, in Upper Canada, on the Fourth of July, 1830.

But although this anniversary affords occasion of rejoicing, to the mass of the people of the United States, there is a class, a numerous class, consisting of nearly three millions, who participate but little in its joys, and are deprived of their unalienable rights, by the very men who so loudly rejoice in the declaration, that "all men are born free and equal."

The festivities of this day serve but to impress upon the minds of reflecting men of colour a deeper sense of the cruelty, the injustice, and oppression of which they have been the victims. While others rejoice in their deliverance from a foreign yoke, they mourn that a yoke a thousandfold more grievous is fastened upon them. Alas, they are slaves in the midst of freeman; they are slaves to those who boast that freedom is the unalienable right of all; and the clanking of their fetters, and the voice of their wrongs make a horrid discord in the songs of freedom which resound through the land.

## A VOICE FROM PHILADELPHIA.

Philadelphia, January 1817.

At a numerous meeting of the people of color, convened at Bethel church, to take into consideration the propriety of remonstrating against the contemplated measure, that is to exile us from the land of our nativity; James Forten was called to the chair, and Russell Parrott appointed secretary. The intent of the meeting having been stated by the chairman, the following resolutions were adopted, without one dissenting voice.

Whereas our ancestors (not of choice) were the first successful cultivators of the wilds of America, we their descendants feel ourselves entitled to participate in the blessings of her luxuriant soil, which their blood and sweat manured; and that any measure or system of measures, having a tendency to banish us from her bosom, would not only be cruel, but in direct violation of those principles, which have been the boast of this republic.

Resolved, That we view with deep abhorrence the unmerited stigma attempted to be cast upon the reputation of the free people of color, by the promoters of this measure, 'that they are a dangerous and useless part of the community,' when in the state of disfranchisement in which they live, in the hour of danger they ceased to remember their wrongs, and rallied around the standard of their country.

Resolved, That we never will separate ourselves voluntarily from the slave population in this country; they are our brethren by the ties of consanguinity, of suffering, and of wrong; and we feel that there is more virtue in suffering privations with them, than fancied advantages for a season.

Resolved, That having the strongest confidence in the justice of God, and philanthropy of the free states, we cheerfully submit our destinies to the guidance of Him who suffers not a sparrow to fall, without his special providence.

Resolved, That a committee of eleven persons be appointed to open a correspondence with the honorable Joseph Hopkinson, member of Congress from this city, and likewise to inform him of the sentiments of this meeting, and that the following named

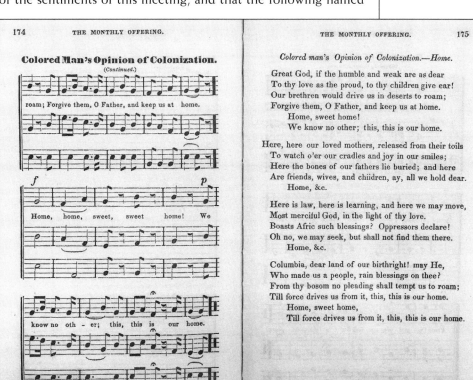

The "Colored Man's Opinion of Colonization" was written to be sung at abolitionist meetings. For many African Americans, the United States was their home and Africa had become a foreign land to which they had no desire to return.

persons constitute the committee, and that they have power to call a general meeting, when they in their judgment may deem it proper.

**David Walker's *Appeal to the Coloured Citizens of the World* (1829) embraced the kind of violent opposition to slavery that was recognized as possible when blacks mobilized. In the late 1820s some blacks were increasingly open in their criticisms of slavery and the white community. Walker often addresses himself to "Americans," meaning those who have perpetuated the systems of racial prejudice and slavery. Although blacks have a right to live freely in the United States, Walker recognizes his people as having an inherently different identity from the community of white Americans. At the same time, however, he demands that whites recognize that blacks are Americans, too, and deserve the rights of Americans.**

**Walker, a used clothing dealer, sewed copies of his pamphlets into some of the coats he sold to seafarers and for the southern market. When copies appeared in southern cities, the pamphlet was banned and those caught with it arrested.**

Americans! notwithstanding you have and do continue to treat us more cruel than any heathen nation ever did a people it had subjected to the same condition that you have us. Now let us reason—

I mean you of the United States, whom I believe God designs to save from destruction, if you will hear. For I declare to you whether you believe it or not, that there are some on the continent of America, who will never be able to repent. God will surely destroy them, to show you his disapprobation of the murders they and you have inflicted on us. I say, let us reason; had you not better take our body, while you have it in your power, and while we are yet ignorant and wretched, not knowing but a little, give us education, and teach us the pure religion of our Lord and Master, which is calculated to make the lion lay down in peace with the lamb, and which millions of you have beaten us nearly to death trying to obtain since we have been among you, and thus at once, gain our affection while we are ignorant? Remember Americans, that we must and shall be free and enlightened as you are, will you wait until we shall, under God, obtain our liberty by the crushing arm of power? Will it not be dreadful for you? I speak Americans for your good. We must and shall be free I say, in spite of you. You may do your best to keep us in wretchedness and misery, to enrich you and your children; but God will deliver us from under you. And wo[e], wo[e] , will be to you if we have to obtain our freedom by fighting. Throw away your fears, and prejudices then, and enlighten us and treat us like men, and we will like you more than we do now hate you, and tell us now no more about colonization, for America is as much our country, as it is yours.—Treat us like men, and there is no danger but we will all live in peace and happiness together. For we are not like you, hard hearted, unmerciful, and unforgiving. What a happy country this will be, if whites will listen. What nation under heaven, will be able to do any thing with us, unless God gives us up into its hand? But Americans, I declare to you, while you keep us and our children in bondage, and treat us like brutes, to make us support you and your families, we cannot be your friends. You do not look for it, do you? Treat us then like men, and we will be your friends. And there is not a doubt in my mind, but that the whole of the past will be sunk into oblivion, and we yet, under God, will become united and happy people. The whites may say it is impossible, but remember that nothing is impossible with God.

The Americans may say or do as they please, but they have to raise us from the condition of brutes to that of respectable men, and to make a national acknowledgment to us for the wrongs they have inflicted on us. As unexpected, strange, and wild as these propositions may to some appear, it is no less a fact, that in less they are complied with, the Americans of the United States, though they may for a little while escape. God will yet weigh them in a balance, and if they are not superior to other men, as they have represented themselves to be, he will give them wretchedness to their very heart's content.

And now brethren, having concluded these four Articles, I submit them, together with my preamble, dedicated to the Lord, for your inspection, in language so very simple, that the most ignorant, who can read at all, may easily understand—of which you may make the best you possibly can. Should tyrants take it into their heads to emancipate any of you, remember that your freedom is your natural right. You are men, as well as they, and instead of returning thanks to them for your freedom, return it to the

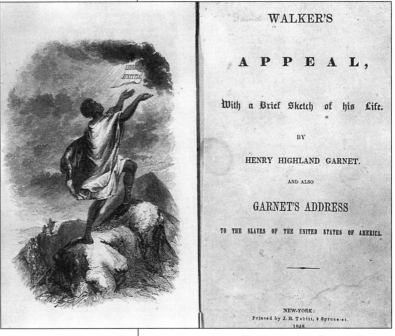

The frontispiece of this 1848 edition of David Walker's Appeal likens him to a biblical figure receiving the words "Liberty" and "Justice" from heaven. Like other abolitionists, Walker argued strongly that true Christians should oppose slavery.

*Caesar, photographed here in 1852, was probably the last slave in New York State. He worked as a house servant. For many freed blacks the distinction between slavery and paid servitude was negligible because their opportunities were limited and their occupations did not always change with their liberation.*

Holy Ghost, who is our rightful owner. If they do not want to part with your labours, which have enriched them, let them keep you and my word for it, that God Almighty, will break their strong band. Do you believe this, my brethren?. . .Whether you believe it or not, I tell you that God will dash tyrants, in combination with devils, into atoms, and will bring you out from your wretchedness and miseries under these *Christian People ! ! ! ! !*

# Free Blacks Speak Out

**Maria Stewart was the first African-American woman to lecture publicly against slavery. Stewart criticizes the myth that blacks are ignorant and lazy, seeing it as an excuse for the white community to relegate them to positions of unskilled and semiskilled labor, as washerwomen, house servants, and manual laborers. Although such jobs were considered necessary and appropriate by northern whites, these positions limited blacks' opportunities and prevented them from gaining a significant public voice. The result was nothing less than a northern extension of black enslavement. Stewart recognizes this white attitude as the most damning northern prejudice because it seeks to prevent the intellectual development of black northerners and, in so doing, impedes the ability of blacks to better themselves from within their own community.**

**Maria Stewart delivered the following lecture at Franklin Hall in Boston on September 21, 1832.**

Methinks I heard a spiritual interrogation—'Who shall go forward and take off the reproach that is cast upon the people of color? Shall it be a woman?' And my heart made this reply—'If it is thy will, be it even so, Lord Jesus!'

I have heard much respecting the horrors of slavery; but may Heaven forbid that the generality of my color throughout these United States should experience any more of its horrors than to be a servant of servants, or hewers of wood and drawers of water [Joshua 9:23]! Tell us no more of southern slavery; for with few exceptions, although I may be very erroneous in my opinion, yet I consider our condition but little better than that. Yet, after all, methinks there are no chains so galling as those that bind the soul, and exclude it from the vast field of useful and scientific knowledge. O, had I received the advantages of an early education, my ideas would, ere now, have expanded far and wide but, alas! I possess nothing but moral capability—no teachings but the teachings of the Holy Spirit.

I have asked several individuals of my sex, who transact business for themselves, if providing our girls were to give them the most satisfactory references, they would not be willing to grant them an equal opportunity with others? Their reply has been—for their own part, they had no objection; but as it was not the custom, were they to take them into their employ, they would be in danger of losing public patronage.

And such is the powerful force of prejudice. Let our girls possess whatever amiable qualities of soul they may; let their characters be fair and spotless as innocence itself; let their natural taste and ingenuity be what they may; it is impossible for scarce and individual of them to rise above the condition of servants. Ah! why is this cruel and unfeeling distinction? Is it merely because God has made our complexion vary? If it be, O shame to soft, relenting humanity! "tell it not in Gath! publish it not in the streets of Askelon!" [2 Samuel 1:20]. Yet, after all, methinks were the American free people of color to turn their attention more assiduously to moral worth and intellectual improvement, this would be the result: prejudice would gradually be diminished, and whites would be compelled to say, unloose those fetters!

Though black their skins as shades of night

Their hearts are pure, their souls are white.

Few white persons of either sex, who are calculated for anything else, are willing to spend their lives and bury their talents in performing mean, servile labor. And such is the horrible idea that I entertain respecting a life of servitude, that if I concieved of [there] being no possibility of my rising above the condition of servants, I would gladly hail death as a welcome messenger. O, horrible idea, indeed! to possess noble souls aspiring after high and honorable acquirements, yet, confined by the chains of ignorance and poverty to lives of continual drudgery and toil. Neither do I know of any who have enriched themselves by spending their lives as house-domestics, washing windows, shaking carpets, brushing boots, or tending upon gentlemen's tables. I can but die for expressing my sentiments; and I am willing to die by the sword as the pestilence, for I am a true born American; your blood flows in my veins, and your spirit fires my breast.

I observed a piece in the *Liberator* a few months since, stating that the colonizationists had published a work respecting us, asserting that we were lazy and idle. I confute them on that point.

*The minds of the blacks are not competent to vote. They are too much degraded to estimate the value, or exercise with fidelity and discretion that important right. It would be unsafe in their hands.*

—Robert Young, the representative from Saratoga, at the 1821 New York State Constitutional Convention

Take us generally as a people, we are neither lazy nor idle; and considering how little we have to excite or stimulate us, I am almost astonished that there are so many industrious and ambitious ones to be found; although I acknowledge, with extreme sorrow, that there are some who never were and never will be serviceable to society. And have you not a similar class among yourselves?

Again. It was asserted that we were "a ragged set, crying for liberty." I reply to it, the whites have so long and so loudly proclaimed them of equal rights and privileges, that our souls have caught the flame also, ragged as we are. As far as our merit deserves, we feel a common desire to rise above the condition of servants and drudges. I have learnt, by bitter experience, that continual hard labor deadens the energies of the soul, and benumbs the faculties of the mind; the ideas become confined, the mind barren, and, like the uncultivated soil, brings forth thorns and thistles. . . .

I do not consider it derogatory, my friends, for persons to live out to service. There are many whose inclination leads them to aspire no higher; and I would highly recommend the performance of almost anything for an honest livelihood; but where constitutional strength is wanting, labor of this kind, in its mildest form, is painful. And doubtless many are the prayers that have ascended to Heaven from Afric's daughters for strength to perform their work. Oh, many are the tears that have been shed for the want of that strength! Most of our color have dragged out a miserable existence of servitude from the cradle to the grave. And what literary acquirement can be made, or useful knowledge derived, from either maps, books, or charts, by those who continually drudge from Monday morning until Sunday noon? O, ye fairer sisters, whose hands are never soiled, whose nerves and muscles are never strained, go learn by experience! Had we had the opportunity that you have had, to improve our moral and mental faculties, what would have hindered our intellects from being as bright, and our manners from being as dignified as yours? Had it been our lot to have been nursed in the lap of affluence and ease, and to have basked beneath the smiles and sunshine of fortune, should we not have naturally supposed that we were never made to toil? And why are not our forms as delicate, and our constitutions as slender, as yours? is not the workmanship as curious and complete? Have pity upon us, have pity upon us, O ye who have hearts to feel for other's woes; for the hand of God has touched us. Owing to the disadvantages under which we labor, there are many flowers among us that are

. . .born to bloom unseen

And waste their fragrance on the desert air.

My beloved brethren, as Christ has died in vain for those who will not accept his offered mercy, so will it be vain for the advocates of freedom to spend their breath in our behalf, unless with united hearts and souls you make some mighty efforts to raise your sons and daughters from the horrible state of servitude and degradation in which they are placed. . . . Look at our young men, smart, active and energetic, with souls filled with ambitious fire; if they look forward, alas! What are their prospects? They can be nothing but the humblest laborers, on account of their dark complexions hence many of them lose their ambition, and become worthless. Look at our middle-aged men, clad in their rusty plaids and coats; in winter, every cent they earn goes to buy their wood and pay their rents; the poor wives also toil beyond their strength, to help support their families. Look at our aged sires, whose heads are whitened with the frosts of seventy winters, with their old wood-saws on their backs. Alas, what keeps us so? Prejudice, ignorance and poverty. But ah! methinks our oppression is soon to come to an end; yea, before the Majesty of heaven, our groans and cries have reached the ears of the Lord of Sabbath [James 5:4]. As the prayers and tears of Christians will avail the finally impenitent nothing; neither will the prayers and tears of the friends of humanity avail us anything, unless we possess a spirit of virtuous emulation within our breasts. Did the pilgrims, when they first landed on these shores, quietly compose themselves and say, "The Britons have all the money and all the power, and we must continue their servants forever?" Did they sluggishly sigh and say, "Our lot is hard, the Indians own the soil, and we cannot cultivate it?" No; they first made powerful efforts to raise themselves, and then God raised up those illustrious patriots, WASHINGTON and LAFAYETTE, to assist and defend them. And, my brethren, have you made a powerful effort? Have you prayed the legislature for mercy's sake to grant you all the rights and privileges of free citizens, that your

This Philadelphia street scene painted by the Russian diplomat Paul Svinin during his 1813–15 travels in the United States reveals some of the occupations that engaged free blacks in the urban North. The occupations depicted—providing childcare, selling firewood, and moving furniture— were fairly typical.

daughters may rise to that degree of respectability which true merit deserves, and your sons above the servile situation which most of them fill?

**By the 1840s, northern free blacks were agitating for the vote. The New York State constitution of 1821 had practically disfranchised African-American men by setting a very high property requirement for black male voters. This particularly angered blacks in New York because black men had held the vote for decades previously, after an earlier convention in 1777. Indeed, in some wards of New York City during the 1810s, black male voters determined the course of elections.**

**When New York's African-American leaders gathered in 1845 to protest their disfranchisement, they were participating in a larger trend, the black convention movement. Beginning in 1840, free blacks attended conventions in various states to debate issues of relevance to the community, such as the vote; to strategize; and to pass resolutions. These resolutions, such as these recorded at the New York State Free Suffrage Convention held September 8, 1845, were distributed as pamphlets and reprinted in the sympathetic (usually abolitionist) newspapers.**

Resolved, That the only thing for which a Government and laws are wanted is, for the protection of man in the rights which God has given him.

Resolved, That equality in the use of the elective franchise is the only true basis of a Democratic Government.

Resolved, That the extension of this right to one portion of the citizens of this State, and the withholding it from another, however small, is a shameful denial of the fundamental doctrines of genuine Republicanism.

Resolved, That the disfranchisement of the colored citizens of New-York was altogether uncalled for, and unjust, as forty-five years of equal suffrage full prove.

Resolved, That the majority, by imposing a property qualification upon colored voters, who are greatly in the minority, while they will not observe the same qualifications among themselves, betrays a spirit of despotism and oppression, which we can find only in the most tyrannical and despotic Governments.

Resolved, That it is hypocritical for the people of this State to complain of oppression in foreign lands, while they are tolerating an invidious constitutional distinction in regard to the fundamental principles of the Government, which holds that all men are created equal.

Resolved, That we find no fault with the laws of the land, which welcome the oppressed of other nations (if they are white) to the benefits of our institutions, and which furnish a safe asylum; but we complain that we, native-born citizens, are denied the same rights which are so largely and freely extended to foreigners.

Resolved, That the town Board of the several towns in this State, upon which is devolved, by the statute, the duty of selecting from the tax lists, suitable jurors for the courts of record of the respective counties, in uniformly rejecting persons of color, without regard to their qualifications or moral worth, have added greatly to the oppressions under which the colored people labor, and have thus given a semi-official sanction to the prevalent wicked prejudice against color, and gratuitously multiplied the disabilities of an injured people.

Resolved, That the property qualification required of colored voters, is unreasonable, unjustifiable, and unnecessary; draws one line of caste between blacks and whites, and another between colored men; and virtually says to the freeholders—Property, not intelligence, integrity, and patriotism, is the measure of the man.

Resolved, That we demand the restoration of our rights, at the hands of the people of the State of New-York, who, without cause, took them from us, and have persisted in the wrong for the last twenty-four years.

Resolved, That to the non-possession of the elective franchise may be traced most of the degradation to which we, as a people, have been subjected, and is the fruitful source of unnumbered and unmitigated civil, literary, and religious wrongs.

Resolved, That in proportion as we are treated with disrespect, contumely, and neglect, in our political, literary, and ecclesiastical relations, from the want of the elective franchise; so would we command respect and influence, in these different relations, by the possession of it.

Resolved, That there is great hope for the politically oppressed, in their own exertions, replying upon the favor of Heaven, and appealing to the just sentiments of those in political power.

Resolved, That we hold the elective franchise as a mighty lever for elevating, in the scale of society, any people, and feel sensible that without it, we are but nominally free, the vital means of our improvement being paralyzed: we do therefore believe it obligatory on us, and do hereby pledge ourselves to each other, to use

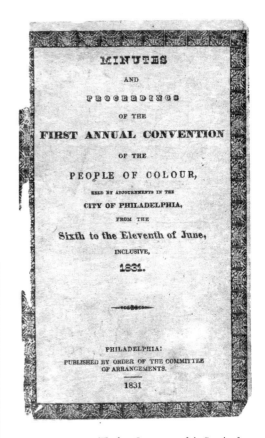

The first Convention of the People of Colour was held for six days in June 1831 in Philadelphia. Among the resolutions passed was one that encouraged blacks to settle in Canada but that opposed colonization in Africa. This convention was the first in a series that became known as the convention movement. This movement was an important arena for blacks to advocate for the end of slavery and other significant reforms.

*The abolitionist press not only published almanacs for adults but also literature for children. Like this alphabet, poems, songs, and stories were used to introduce young readers to antislavery themes. Children were also encouraged to raise money for the antislavery cause.*

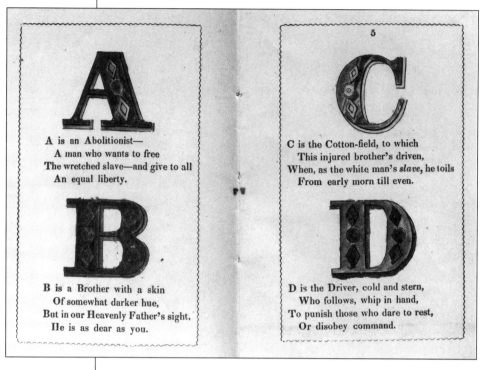

all just means in our power, by devoting a portion of our time, talent, and substance, to agitate this question, until we obtain a restoration of this inestimable boon.

Resolved, That in case a Convention should be called, it is the duty of every friend of equal suffrage to vote for those delegates, in the Whig or Democratic parties, that are in favor of extending to the colored people of this state, equal suffrage.

## Another Independence Day

**Many of the subscribers to the abolitionist press—and many of its writers—were African Americans. Not surprisingly, their eloquent critiques of slavery and racial prejudice were banned in the South, leading antislavery northerners to add "free speech" to their list of reasons why northern society was more truly American than the South.**

**Peter Osborne, a black leader from New Haven, Connecticut, began his 1832 speech by explaining why black and white abolitionists were celebrating Independence Day on the fifth of July. By that year, blacks had begun to hold alternative celebrations to July Fourth in order to protest their exclusion from American citizenship (and from the actual festive activities). Much of the language of Osborne's speech**

**survived into the civil rights struggle of the next century—
including the closing injunction to keep our eyes on the
"prize" of liberty and equal rights.**

Fellow-Citizens—On account of misfortune of our color, our
fourth of July comes on the fifth; but I hope and trust that when
the Declaration of Independence is fully executed, which declares
that all men, without respect to person, were born free and equal,
we may then have our fourth of July on the fourth. It is thought
by many that this is impossible to take place, as it is for the leop-
ard to change his spots; but I anticipate that the time is approach-
ing very fast. The signs in the north, the signs in the south, in the
east and west, are all favorable to our cause. Why, then, should we
forbear contending for the civil rights of free country-men? What
man of national feeling would slumber in content under the yoke
of slavery and oppression, in his own country? Not the most
degraded barbarian in the interior of Africa.

If we desire to see our brethren relieved from the tyrannical
yoke of slavery and oppression in the south, if we would enjoy the
civil rights of free countrymen, it is high time for us to be up and
doing. It has been said that we have already done well, but we can
do better. What more can we do? Why, we must unite with our
brethren in the north, in the south, and in the east and west, and
then with the Declaration of Independence in one hand, and the
Holy Bible in the other, I think we might courageously give battle to the most powerful enemy to this cause. The Declaration of
Independence has declared to man, without speaking to color,
that all men are born free and equal. Has it not declared this freedom and equality to us too?

What man would content himself, and say nothing of the
rights of man, with two million of his brethren in bondage? Let us
contend for the prize. Let us all unite, and with one accord declare
that we will not leave our country to emigrate to Liberia, nor elsewhere, to be civilized nor christianized. Let us make known to
America that we are not barbarians; that we are not inhuman
beings; that this is our native country; that our forefathers have
planted trees in America for us, and we intend to stay and eat the
fruit. Our forefathers fought, bled and died to achieve independence of the United States. Why should we forbear contending
for the prize? It becomes every colored citizen in the United
States to step forward boldly, and gallantly defend his rights.
What has there been done within a few years, since the union of
the colored people? Are we not gaining ground? Yes—and had we

begun this work forty years ago, I do not hesitate to say that there would not have been, at this day, a slave in the United States. Take, courage, then, ye Afric-Americans! Don't give up the conflict, for the glorious prize can be won.

**Frederick Douglass was the most important African-American leader of the 19th century. He was an escaped slave from Maryland who lectured to abolitionists, published a narrative of his life in the South, and then started his own newspaper, in Rochester, New York. In 1852 he was invited to give an address on July 5 to local abolitionists who had boycotted the July Fourth celebration. His speech that day remains one of the most eloquent protests against both slavery and the denial of civil rights to the emancipated. It is also a reflection on what it was like to be a black activist in the 1850s, after the Fugitive Slave Law required runaway slaves to be returned to their owners even if they fled north. Douglass's call for "scorching irony," and his use of such angry ridicule, shows that he had profited from studying the speaking and writing strategies of his free black predecessors, such as Henry Sipkins, Peter Williams, David Walker, and Maria Stewart.**

FELLOW-CITIZENS——pardon me, and allow me to ask, why am I called upon to speak here to-day? What have I, or those I represent, to do with your national independence? Are the great principles of political freedom and of natural justice, embodied in that Declaration of Independence, extended to us? and am I, therefore, called upon to bring our humble offering to the national altar, and to confess the benefits, and express devout gratitude for the blessing, resulting from your independence to us?

Would to God, both for your sakes and ours, that an affirmative answer could be truthfully returned to these questions! Then would my task be light, and my burden easy and delightful. For who is there so cold that a nation's sympathy could not warm him? Who so obdurate and dead to the claims of gratitude, that would not thankfully acknowledge such priceless benefits? Who so stolid and selfish, that would not give his voice to swell the hallelujahs of a nation's jubilee, when the chains of servitude had been torn from his limbs? I am not that man. In a case like that, the dumb might eloquently speak, and the "lame man leap as an hart."

But, such is not the state of the case. I say it with a sad sense of the disparity between us. I am not included within the pale of this glorious anniversary! Your high independence only reveals the immeasurable distance between us. The blessing in which you this day rejoice, are not enjoyed in common. The rich inheritance of justice, liberty, prosperity, and independence, bequeathed by your fathers, is shared by you, not by me. The sunlight that brought life and healing to you, has brought stripes and death to me. This Fourth of July is *yours*, not *mine*. *You* may rejoice, *I* must mourn. To drag a man in fetters into the grand illuminated temple of liberty, and call upon him to join you in joyous anthems, were inhuman mockery and sacrilegious irony. . . . My subject, then, fellow citizens, is AMERICAN SLAVERY. I shall see this day and its popular characteristics from the slave's point of view. Standing there, identified with the American bondman, making his wrongs mine. I do not hesitate to declare, with all my soul, that the character and conduct of this nation never looked blacker to me than on this Fourth of July. Whether we turn to the declarations of the past, or to the professions of the present, the conduct of the nation seems equally hideous and revolting. America is false to the past, false to the present, and solemnly binds herself to be false to the future. Standing with God and the crushed and bleeding slave on this occasion, I will, in the name of humanity which is outraged, in the name of liberty which is fettered, in the name of the constitution and the bible, which are disregarded and trampled upon, dare to call in question and to denounce, with all the emphasis I can command, everything that serves to perpetuate slavery—the great sin and shame of America! "I will not equivocate; I will not excuse;" I will use the severest language I can command; and yet not one word shall escape me that any man whose judgment is not blinded by prejudice, or who is not at heart a slaveholder, shall not confess to be right and just.

But I fancy I hear some one of my audience say, it is just in this circumstance that you and your brother abolitionists fail to make a favorable impression on the public mind. Would you argue more, and denounce less, would you persuade more and rebuke less, your cause would be much more likely to succeed. But, I submit, where all is plain there is nothing to be argued. What point in the anti-slavery creed would you have me argue? On what branch of the subject do the people of this country need light? Must I undertake to prove that the slave is a man? That point is conceded already. Nobody doubts it. The slaveholders themselves acknowledge it in the enactment of laws of their government. They acknowledge it when they punish disobedience on the part

At a time when gift books were valued possessions, Douglass and other famous abolitionists often autographed their books to raise funds. The "something more" is a stirring example of Frederick Douglass's use of language to further the antislavery cause. The repetition of the phrase "I am for liberty" is an example of the oratorical style that was later used so effectively by Martin Luther King, Jr., in his "I Have a Dream" speech.

of the slave. There are seventy-two crimes in the state of Virginia, which, if committed by a black man, (no matter how ignorant he be,) subject him to the punishment of death; while only two of these same crimes will subject a white man to the like punishment. What is this but the acknowledgment that the slave is a moral, intellectual, and responsible being. The manhood of the slave is conceded. It is admitted in the fact that southern statute books are covered with enactments forbidding, under severe fines and penalties, the teaching of the slave to read or write. When you can point to any such laws, in reference to the beasts of the field, then I may consent to argue the manhood of the slave. When the dogs in your streets, when the fowls of the air, when the cattle on your hills, when the fish of the sea, and the reptiles that crawl, shall be unable to distinguish the slave from a brute, then will I argue with you that the slave is a man! . . .

Would you have me argue that man is entitled to liberty? that he is the rightful owner of his own body? You have already declared it. Must I argue the wrongfulness of slavery? Is that a question for republicans? Is it to be settled by the rules of logic and argumentation, as a matter beset with great difficulty, involving a doubtful application of the principle of justice, hard to be understood? How should I look to-day in the presence of Americans, dividing and subdividing a discourse, to show that men have a natural right to freedom, speaking of it relatively and positively, negatively and affirmatively? To do so, would be to make myself ridiculous, and to offer an insult to your understanding. There is not a man beneath the canopy of heaven that does not know that slavery is wrong *for him*.

What! am I to argue that it is wrong to make men brutes, to rob them of their liberty, to work them without wages, to keep them ignorant of their relations to their fellow-men, to beat them with sticks, to flay their flesh with the lash, to load their limbs with irons, to hunt them with dogs, to sell them at auction, to sunder their families, to knock out their teeth, to burn their flesh, to starve them into obedience and submission to their masters? Must I argue that a system, thus marked with blood and stained with pollution, is wrong? No; I will not. I have better employment for my time and strength than such arguments would imply.

What, then, remains to be argued? Is it that slavery is not divine; that God did not establish it; that our doctors of divinity are mistaken? There is blasphemy in the thought. That which is inhuman cannot be divine. Who can reason on such a proposition! They that can, may; I cannot. The time for such argument is past.

At a time like this, scorching irony, not convincing argument, is needed. Oh! had I the ability, and could I reach the nation's ear, I would to-day pour out a fiery stream of biting ridicule, blasting reproach, withering sarcasm, and stern rebuke. For it is not light that is needed, but fire; it is not the gentle shower, but thunder. We need the storm, the whirlwind, and the earthquake. The feeling of the nation must be quickened; the conscience of the nation must be roused; the propriety of the nation must be startled; the hypocrisy of the nation must be exposed; and its crimes against God and man must be proclaimed and denounced.

What to the American slave is your Fourth of July? I answer, a day that reveals to him, more than all other days in the year, the gross injustice and cruelty to which he is the constant victim. To him, your celebration is a sham; your boasted liberty, an unholy license; your national greatness, swelling vanity; your sounds of rejoicing are empty and heartless; your denunciations of tyrants, brass-fronted impudence; your shouts of liberty and equality, hollow mockery; your prayers and hymns, your sermons and thanksgiving, with all your religious parade and solemnity, are to him mere bombast, fraud, deception, impiety, and hypocrisy—a thin veil to cover up crimes which would disgrace a nation of savages. There is not a nation on earth guilty of practices more shocking and bloody, than are the people of these United States, at this very hour.

## The Call for Civil Rights

**Elizabeth Jennings's account of northern segregation, published in the *New York Tribune* in July 1854, describes an early version of the prejudice experienced (and opposed) by Rosa Parks during the 1950s civil rights movement, when Parks refused to move to the back of a segregated bus in Birmingham, Alabama, thus sparking a successful boycott of the city bus system. Jennings's story clearly demonstrates that legally sanctioned northern prejudice existed; this incident occurred in New York City, not New Orleans, Charleston, or Atlanta. Her personal chronicle makes brutally clear why African Americans needed their own social organizations. Despite the abolition of the slave trade and of northern slavery, northern blacks had little outside protection from racism and prejudice. Increasingly, they had to seek a stable support system within their own community, rather than in the political and legal institutions of white America.**

Sarah E. Adams and myself walked down to the corner of Pearl and Chatham Sts. to take the Third Ave. cars. I held up my hand to the driver and he stopped the cars, we got on the platform, when the conductor told us to wait for the next car; I told him I could not wait, as I was in a hurry to go to church (the other car was about a block off). He told me that the other car had my people in it, that it was appropriated for that purpose. I then told him I had no people. It was no particular occasion; I wished to go to church, as I had been going for the last six months, and I did not wish to be detained. He insisted upon my getting off the car; I told him I would wait on the car until the other car came up; he again insisted on my waiting in the street, but I did not get off the car; by this time the other car came up, and I asked the driver if there was any room in his car. He told me very distinctly, "No, that there was more room in my car than there was in his." Yet this did not satisfy the conductor; he still kept driving me out or off of the car; said he had as much time as I had and could wait just as long. I replied, "Very well, we'll see." He waited some few minutes, when the drivers becoming impatient, he said to me, "Well, you may go in, but remember, if the passengers raise any objections you shall go out, whether or no, or I'll put you out." I answered again and told him I was a respectable person, born and raised in New York, did not know where he was born, that I had never been insulted before while going to church, and that he was a good for nothing impudent fellow for insulting decent persons while on their way to church. He then said I should come out and he would put me out. I told him not to lay his hands on me; he took hold of me and I took hold of his coat and held onto that, he also broke my grasp from that (but previously he had dragged my companion out, she all the while screaming for him to let go). He then ordered the driver to fasten his horses, which he did, and come and help him put me out of the car; they then both seized hold of me by the arms and pulled and dragged me flat down on the bottom of the platform, so that my feet hung one way and my head the other, nearly on the ground. I screamed murder with all my voice, and my companion screamed out "you'll kill her; don't kill her." The driver then let go of me and went to his horses; I went again in the car, and the conductor said you shall sweat for this; then told the driver to drive as fast as he could and not to take another passenger in the car; to drive until he saw an officer or a Station House. They got an officer on the corner of Walker and Bowery, whom the conductor told that his orders from the agent were to admit colored persons if the passengers did not object, but if they did, not to let them ride. When the officer took me there were some eight or ten persons in the car. Then the officer, without listening to anything I had to say, thrust me out, and then pushed me, and tauntingly told me to get redress if I could; this the conductor also told me, and gave me some name and number of his car; he wrote his name Moss and the car No. 7, but I looked and saw No. 6 on the back on the car. After dragging me off the car he drove me away like a dog, saying not to be talking there and raising a mob or fight. I came home down Walker St., and a German gentleman followed, who told me he saw the whole transaction in the street as he was passing; his address is Latour, No. 148 Pearl St., bookseller. When I told the conductor I did not know where he was born, he answered, "I was born in Ireland." I made answer it made no difference where a man was born, that he was none the worse or better for that, provided he behaved himself and did not insult genteel persons.

I would have come up myself, but am quite sore and stiff from the treatment I received from those monsters in human form yesterday afternoon. This statement I believe to be correct, and it is respectfully submitted.

ELIZABETH JENNINGS

John Roberts's letter to his former master, published in the *Toronto Christian Guardian* shows how newspapers were used to publicize opposing views of slavery. It was not uncommon for southern slave owners to appeal publicly to their runaway slaves in newspaper advertisements, claiming that they should return because the conditions of slavery were easier than being free. These appeals sought to combat the accounts that runaways shared with people once they escaped. Roberts's letter from Canada responds to his former master's letter published in a New York newspaper, and it is scathing in its sarcasm and condemnation.

*The growing free black population in the North was not always met with enthusiasm. This 1863 engraving in which well-dressed blacks crowd anxious-looking whites from the Fifth Avenue sidewalk in New York City reveals the fear that some whites felt as blacks asserted themselves in northern society.*

Toronto, Upper Canada                              July 8, 1837

Sir:

I have seen in the Rochester *Democrat* of the Fourth of July, your publication inviting me again to assume the bonds of a Slave. And can you think, that I would voluntarily relinquish Freedom, fully secured to me by the British Government, to return to American Slavery, the vilest that now crushes man and defies God? Is this the appreciation you have of Liberty? If so, I value it more highly. No, Sir, dear to me as are the thoughts of my wife and child, I cannot again become a Slave, if this be the price at which I must purchase the enjoyment of their Society. For them would I freely expend me life—but to become a Slave again! no, never. To ask it, is an insult to the spirit of Liberty, to the Dignity of human nature, to that Heaven born religion you profess.

You say that with "an excellent character for integrity, stability, and sobriety," I have served you "upwards of twenty years." And does this expenditure of my primest manhood entitle me to no reward in my declining years? Send me, then, my wife, my child. Disproportioned as would be the cost of doing this, to the value of the services I have rendered you, 'tis all I ask; it shall by your full acquittance. From one who feels anything of the power of the religion you profess—or who has any touch of humanity, or any regard for justice, I could not ask less, nor would he think of performing less.

You seem to doubt the *sincerity* of the friend, by whose aid I have been enabled to achieve my liberty. How has the habit of oppression warped your judgment and dulled your sensibilities—that you should suspect the motives of those who strike from the helpless Slave his long worn chains. Take it to yourself: what would you think of the friendship of him who, at the hazard of all things, should deliver you or your child from Moorish or Algerine bondage? Would you be so ungrateful as to suspect his motives, when you were a beggar in all things but in thanks? No: you would not. And you would feel a generous indignation, too, against the frozen-hearted traducer who would persuade you to suspect his sincerity. If you should ever be so unfortunate as to be in Slavery, may you find those who will deliver you as I have been delivered—who will make you, as I am made a FREEMAN. *Then*, you will acknowledge their worth,, and know how to honour their friendship. Farewell, Sir, may you enjoy the happiness of those who strive to make others happy,

JOHN ROBERTS

**Many free black leaders returned to the idea of colonization
during the 1850s out of disappointment with the persistence
of slavery in the South and racism in the North. Chief among
them was Martin Robison Delany, a physician and writer who
published a book, *The Condition, Elevation, Emigration, and
Destiny of the Colored People of the United States,* in 1852.
His ideas grew out of the discussion of such black political
strategies during the post–Revolutionary period. Through
social organizations, public lectures, and newspaper publications, a new black nationalism and desire for self-determina-
tion had been created. Delany reflects and promotes an
African-centered view of black (and American) history. He
insists that it is not free blacks who have to work harder to
achieve equality, but rather all whites—including the abolitionists themselves. Why had not abolitionism translated
into better jobs for blacks, for example? In fighting white
efforts to silence black voices, black northern activists created a sense of solidarity and purpose.**

It should be borne in mind, that Anti-Slavery took its rise among
*colored men,* just at the time they were introducing their greatest
projects for their own elevation, and that our Anti-Slavery
brethren were converts of the colored men, in behalf of their elevation. Of course, it would be expected that being baptized into
the new doctrines, their faith would induce them to embrace the
principles therein contained, with the strictest possible adherence.

The cause of dissatisfaction with our former condition, was,
that we were proscribed, debarred, and shut out from every
respectable position, occupying the places of inferiors and menials.

It was expected that Anti-Slavery, according to its professions,
would extend to colored persons, as far as in the power of its
adherents, those advantages nowhere else to be obtained among
white men. That colored boys would get situations in their shops
and stores, and every other advantage tending to elevate them as
far as possible, would be extended to them. At least, it was expected, that in Anti-Slavery establishments, colored men would have
the preference. Because, there was no other ostensible object in
view, in the commencement of the Anti-Slavery enterprise, than
the *elevation* of the *colored man,* by facilitating his efforts in attaining
to equality with the white man. It was urged, and it was true, that
the colored people were susceptible of all that the whites were,
and all that was required was to give them a fair opportunity, and
they would prove their capacity. That it was unjust, wicked, and

cruel, the result of an unnatural prejudice, that debarred them from places of respectability, and that public opinion could and should be corrected upon this subject. That it was only necessary to make a sacrifice of feeling, and an innovation on the customs of society, to establish a different order of things,—that as Anti-Slavery men, they were willing to make these sacrifices, and determined to take the colored man by the hand, making common cause with him in affliction, and bear a part of the odium heaped upon him. That his cause was the cause of God—that "In as much as ye did it not unto the least of these my little ones, ye did it not unto me," and that as Anti-Slavery men, they would "do right if the heavens fell." Thus, was the cause espoused, and thus did we expect much. But in all this, we were doomed to disappointment, sad, sad disappointment. Instead of realising what we had hoped for, we find ourselves occupying the very same position in relation to our Anti-Slavery friends, as we do in relation to the pro-slavery part of the community—a mere secondary, underling position, in all our relations to them, and any thing more than this, is not a matter of course affair—it comes not by established anti-slavery custom or right, but like that which emanates from the proslavery portion of the community, by mere sufferance.

It is true, that the "Liberator" office, in Boston has got Elijah Smith, a colored youth, at the cases—the "Standard," in New York, a young colored man, and the "Freeman," in Philadelphia, William Still, another, in the publication office, as "packing clerk;" yet these are but three out of the hosts that fill these offices in their various departments, all occupying places that could have been, and as we once thought, would have been, easily enough, occupied by colored men. Indeed, we can have no other idea about anti-slavery in this country, than that the legitimate persons to fill any and every position about an anti-slavery establishment are colored persons. Nor will it do to argue in extenuation, that white men are as justly entitled to them as colored men; because white men do not from *necessity* become anti-slavery men in order to get situations; they being white men, may occupy any position they are capable of filling—in a word, their chances are endless, every avenue in the country being opened to them. They do not therefore become abolitionists, for the sake of employment—at least, it is not the song that anti-slavery sung, in the first love of the new faith, proclaimed by its disciples.

And if it be urged that colored men are incapable as yet to fill these positions, all that we have to say is, that the cause has fallen far short; almost equivalent to a failure, of a tithe, of what it

*In this 1858 painting, Moses, a free black, sells the* Baltimore News. *Although in the 19th century blacks found freedom from slavery in the North, free blacks' freedom was limited by the lack of opportunity to advance economically and socially.*

This formal portrait of the Philadelphia Anti-Slavery Society taken in 1851 features prominent abolitionists, such as Lucretia and James Mott, seated at bottom right. The antislavery societies often failed to promote African Americans as leaders, a fact that black members debated publicly and took as a sign that it was necessary for them to continue to have their own separate institutions even while they worked with white supporters.

promised to do in half the period of its existence, to this time, if it have not as yet, now a period of twenty years, raised up colored men enough, to fill the offices within its patronage. We think it is not unkind to say, if it had been half as faithful to itself, as it should have been—its professed principles we mean; it could have reared and tutored from childhood, colored men enough by this time, for its own especial purpose. These we know could have been easily obtained, because colored people in general, are favorable to the anti-slavery cause, and wherever there is an adverse manifestation, it arises from sheer ignorance; and we have now but comparatively few such among us. There is one thing certain, that no colored person, except such as would reject education altogether, would be adverse to putting their child with an anti-slavery person, for educational advantages. This then, could have been done. But it has not been done, and let the cause of it be whatever it may, and let whoever may be to blame, we are willing to let all that pass, and extend to our anti-slavery brethren the right-hand of fellowship, bidding them God-speed in the propagation of good and wholesome sentiments—for whether they are practically carried out or not, the professions are in themselves all right and good. Like Christianity, the principles are holy and of divine origin. And we believe, if ever a man started right, with pure and holy motives, Mr. Garrison did; and that, had he the power of making the cause what it should be, it would all be right, and there never would have been any cause for the remarks we have made, though in kindness, and with the purest of motives. We are nevertheless, still occupying a miserable position in the community, wherever we live; and what we most desire is, to draw the attention of our people to this fact, and point out what, in our opinion, we conceive to be a proper remedy.

*Chapter Four: Picture Essay*

# Slavery and Freedom: Dressing the Part

The debate over slavery took place in print, and by the late 18th century, printers had found inexpensive ways to include drawings in books and pamphlets. These visual images were used to influence public opinion regarding slavery's place in the United States. During the years of the antislavery movement, a variety of technologies—especially the steam press, lithography, and, by the 1850s, photography—allowed people who opposed slavery to add visual images to the verbal pictures of slavery they created in their narratives, speeches, and essays.

The images in this chapter include some of the most effective examples of antislavery and pro-slavery (or anti-abolitionist) pictures from the 1830s to the 1860s. These images often focus on the figure of the slave—and the former slave. What did slaves, and slavery, look like? What did a slave turned free man look like?

Then as now, Americans made statements about who they were through their clothes. Clothes display ownership of one's body and the ability to do what one pleased, and abolitionists knew that one of the marks of the American slave was the particular—often skimpy and shoddy—clothes provided by the master. Although, in reality, slaves often found ways to express themselves through improvised clothing and hairstyles, the image of slavery presented by abolitionists was that of a people who lacked good clothing, in contrast to those who had the ability to dress according to the formal fashions of the day. Therefore, images of slaves and former slaves turned freemen often dramatized the difference in status through changes in clothing.

The Anti-Slavery Almanac *was an annual publication containing calendars and other useful information that the abolitionists sold to raise money. This illustration from the cover of the 1840 almanac satirizes "northern hospitality" in the form of New York's nine month law that permitted temporary residence by slaveowners and their slaves. The slave is depicted as well-dressed, but his lack of shoes and hat and his frayed trousers differentiate him from his enslavers.*

Defenders of slavery responded to accusations of cruelty by insisting that most slaves were well cared for and, in fact, happy. The images in the 1853 version of John Pendleton Kennedy's novel *Swallow Barn* showed well-dressed house slaves being cared for by white and black parents and field slaves looking contented in their long shirts and frayed dresses.

THE FRUITS OF AMALGAMATION.

*Publ.d by JOHN CHILDS. 160¼ Fulton St New York.*

Some white northerners argued that giving free blacks equal rights would lead to "amalgamation," or intermarriage, and black power over whites. This lithograph, entitled "The Fruits of Amalgamation" (1839), depicts whites as servants to blacks, who lounge in fancy clothes.

Solomon Northup was kidnapped by slave traders and worked on a Red River plantation in Louisiana. In 1853 he published a narrative, *Twelve Years a Slave*. The title page illustrates Northup in his shabby "plantation suit," which marks his identity as a slave.

By contrast to Solomon Northup's portrait, the frontispiece of the *Narrative of the Life of Frederick Douglass* (1845)—the slave who had freed himself—shows a man who, when he could, dressed himself neatly and fashionably.

Engraved by J.C.Buttre

*Frederick Douglass*

These Frederick Douglass dolls were made by Cynthia Hill of New Bedford, Massachusetts, during the late 1850s. The dolls' costumes celebrate Douglass's transformation from slavery to freedom. Douglass the slave wears the loose-fitting clothes associated with servants and children. The free Douglass wears fitted clothing, a jacket and waistcoat. For decades Douglass served as an embodiment of freedom's potential, as well as a spokesman for African Americans.

This 1855 flyer traces the story of captured fugitive Anthony Burns from his original escape from slavery, to his life as a working man in Boston, to his arrest, to his address to an abolitionist meeting and emergence as an antislavery hero, to his extradition and resale in the South. At each stage of his story, Burns' clothes signify his status as a slave or freeman.

Light-skinned Ellen Craft escaped from slavery dressed as an older white man, accompanied by her husband, William, who posed as her slave. This portrait of Ellen Craft first appeared in their memoir *Running a Thousand Miles for Freedom* (1860).

AS WE FOUND THEM.

These children were owned by Thomas White, of Mathews Co. Va., until Feb. 20th, when Capt. Riley, 6th U. S. C. I., took them and gave them to the Society of Friends to educate at the Orphan's Shelter, Philadelphia.

Profits from sale, for the benefit of the children.

AS THEY ARE NOW.

The Mother of these children was beaten, branded and sold at auction because she was kind to Union Soldiers. As she left for Richmond, Va., Feb. 13th, 1864, bound down in a cart, she prayed "O! God send the Yankees to take my children away."

Profits from sale, for the benefit of the children.

These photographs—probably taken the same day—depicting two slave children "As We Found Them" and "As They Are Now" were sold by abolitionists to raise money for the cause. The exaggerated tatters of the childrens' slave clothes contrast with the neat, respectable clothes provided by their abolitionist benefactors.

Black soldiers in the Civil War proved very proud of their uniforms as symbols of their freedom and their participation in the fight against slavery. Images of black soldiers during the war—whether group portraits like this recruiting poster or individual photographs the soldiers sent to their loved ones—usually include the full uniform.

*Chapter Five*

# The Continual Struggle: Southern Slaves and Masters

J ust as opposition to slavery in the North took many forms, so did the struggle for power between southern slaves and their masters. As with any struggle, there are at least two sides of the story to be told; in this case, both slaves and masters described forms of slave resistance that shaped the very nature of southern society.

The slave resistance most feared by southern white masters was organized rebellion. Although rebellion was not the most common, or necessarily the most effective, method of resistance, threats of revolt received an enormous amount of attention from white southerners. Both slaves and masters were well aware that, in states such as South Carolina and Mississippi, slaves constituted 55 percent of the population, and in some counties even more. Throughout the entire South, slaves made up a substantial part of society. Field slaves posed a particular threat because they were a large and relatively unsupervised group. On night visits to other plantations, an activity that was often forbidden and resulted in punishment, these slaves could spread information with remarkable speed. House slaves, in turn, knew the details of their masters' everyday lives and could spread information even by day, while on errands or in the course of other tasks. By entrusting the care of their farms and their lives to slaves, masters created the conditions that made revolt an ever-present possibility. The best evidence of this threat is not the number of revolts planned or executed. It is the many waves of panic that swept the South, especially after Denmark Vesey's attempted uprising in South Carolina in 1822, and the rise of the call for immediate abolition from some antislavery northerners after 1830.

*African Americans were central to many white plantation families because of their daily presence in plantation homes.*

*Tags such as this servant's badge from 1823 were used to identify free blacks and slaves. White southerners' fear of rebellion resulted in harsh measures to restrict the movement all African Americans, even those who were "free."*

Southern leaders passed laws that made it illegal for slaves to read or to gather together, continuing the trend that began in the wake of slave conspiracies during the colonial era. They also silenced worrisome dissent, including any criticisms of slavery by whites, through the courts and by mobs who were allowed to commit acts of violence while the authorities looked the other way. In addition, slave patrols (often staffed by non-slaveholding whites), responsible for checking passes and searching for fugitives, roved the countryside. Given these conditions, the antebellum South (the South before the Civil War) no longer appears to have been the simple premodern agricultural society depicted in novels and movies during the early 20th century. Rather, it looks like a police state, in which ordinary adults are kept under constant surveillance and punished or killed if they break the rules.

Fugitive slaves told stories of how difficult it had been for them to escape the oversight of rich and poor whites and make their way north to freedom. Because of slave patrols and the rural nature of the South, individual acts of running away proved more effective than group escapes or organized rebellions in gaining freedom. And yet masters were right to sense that individual acts of fleeing were something more than random, isolated events— something that abolitionists, in their speeches and publications, never let them forget. The regularity of running away, and the occasional acts of violence against masters, proved that slaves were people who wanted freedom. They were not happy as slaves, despite the attempts of slavery advocates to prove that they were better-off than white wage earners in the North or their contemporaries in Africa.

Despite the attention rebellions received, the power of everyday resistance created a much greater, and more subversive, threat to white society. These examples of daily, personal resistance reveal a slave population that was able to act—to take advantage of its proximity to white masters. The role of house slaves was particularly important, and many slaves worked within the household. Only a small minority of southern whites owned plantations with more than 20 slaves. The stereotype of huge plantations with hundreds of field-workers is not wholly accurate, though such places certainly existed. Although they lacked privacy, slaves who lived and worked in the house had access to many resources, and they utilized their position to resist their masters in crucial ways.

Both master and slave accounts of the antebellum South describe everyday acts of resistance. Although whites recalled these instances as an opportunity to reassert power and punish slaves, their testimonies also suggest that slaves gained a measure of control through these sometimes subtle refusals to obey their masters. The connection between these ordinary events and the fear of widespread rebellion is significant. House slaves (and some field slaves as well) represented the potential power of a unified slave population, a possibility that spurred the white obsession with controlling slave activities.

Slave narratives and testimonials describe a similar resistance. These accounts reveal a horror of slave life that is absent from white recollections, however. These narratives, although true stories, are written in a self-conscious manner. They appeal to both a white northern audience and a southern audience. In describing personal experiences and successful resistance, slave narratives functioned in three distinct ways. They presented a reality of slave life to northern audiences who were told by southern writers that the slave population was contented. Slave narratives also were themselves examples of ultimately successful everyday resistance: they demonstrated that escape was possible. The narratives also showed that learning to read and write was possible, despite the laws against teaching slaves. Finally, these narratives described a powerful slave threat that could not be mastered by white southerners. Although personal freedom could be denied, and organized gatherings could be outlawed, white dependence on blacks permitted the possibility of personal, daily resistance by slaves. This kind of resistance could be regulated, but it could not be prevented.

The multiple views of slave power and slave resistance describe a divided South, one in which the white masters were not always in control. In considering the differing stories of slaves and masters, one point becomes clear. Despite the masters' insistence that slaves were happy, an underlying fear of, and anger at, slave resistance pervaded their lives. Southern slaves manipulated their positions to feign contentment as they simultaneously resisted their masters on a regular basis.

# Private and Public Rebellion

**The diary of Landon Carter, a white Virginian slaveholder of the late 18th century, recounts a seemingly ordinary event in the life of a southern house slave. Many house slaves, unlike field-workers, had regular contact with members of the southern white elite. As Carter's entry reveals, the potential dishonesty of house slaves posed a threat to southerners.**

**Despite the reality of tyrannical punishment, slaves such as Sukey often succeeded in their personal rebellions against plantation masters. The intimacy of relations meant that slaves could learn how to manipulate masters; they could play members of the white family against each other or gain their respect and an admission that slaves had certain rights as well as responsibilities.**

**One of these rights was the limited right to have their own families. In documents like Carter's diary, slave owners describe slaves as possessions, using terms such as "my people" or "my black family," but they also admit that black men and women were committed to their own spouses and children, as when Carter refers to "Juba's Harry." On plantations especially, large interlocking slave families could gain special rights—and opportunities to help themselves and each other—because of their relations. The drama recounted by Carter involves a great deal of trust and mistrust and a certain sense that some people are more believable, and deserve better treatment for themselves and their kin, because of a long history within the plantation household.**

*22. Tuesday.*

Last night just as we were going to the Girl, old Sukey's Granddaughter came up and shewed a bloody ear which she said John Selfe's [the overseer's] wife with whom she lives had Stuck pins in. My fellow Daniel came also up and said John Selfe was going to whip him about some corn which he said was lost out of the landing warehouse, when Selfe's wife had left [the key?] in the door, but he knew nothing about it. These 2 stories made me suspend my conclusion until I could hear farther about it.

This morning, seeing no Pinholes in that girl's ear only some blood about it, I asked her why she said the woman had run pins into it. She stood still for some time, and at last told me the overseer had whipped her about giving the Warehouse key to Jubas Harry; and her Granny bid her come and tell me that Selfe's wife had run pins into it; but begged Granny might not know that she told that she bid her say so, or she would whip her for it. After this, I asked Selfe how he came to whip her over the ear. He said that was an accident which he was sorry for, though she certainly deserved to be whipped, for he always kept that Key locked up in his chest, but that day left it with his wife to lock her soap tub which she had just made in the warehouse; and going to the landing to catch a few crabs, the girl in the meantime took the key off

## Roasted Cowhide

*Mattie J. Jackson remembered her early childhood as a slave and published a memoir after the Civil War.*

When we first went to Mr. L's they had a cowhide which she used to inflict on a little slave girl she previously owned, nearly every night. This was done to learn the little girl to wake early to wait on her children. But my mother was a cook, as I before stated, and was in the habit of roasting meats and toasting bread. As they stinted us for food my mother roasted the cowhide. It was rather poor picking, but it was the last cowhide my mother ever had an opportunity to cook while we remained in his family.

Sabine Hall was the main house of Colonel Landon Carter's plantation. The Greek Revival style of architecture, with its distinctive columns and porticoes, in which Sabine Hall was built was popular during the late 18th and early 19th centuries.

the chest and gave it to Jubas Harry, and he went in with Daniel and took out corn enough for both them he did suppose at least a week's allowance each of them.

However my good folks at home from their old heaven ever shewn to me in the most ungrateful of instances, beleived every tittle of the above story as the Girl last night at first related it. And at breakfast I had a most agreeable Peal about the impudence of John Selfe and his prodigeous barbarity which these few drops of blood on the Ear of a child in every instance very fat and Cleanly. Something so inconstant made me angry, and I was then asked what I had to say about Selfe's threatening to shoot my Son's something because he had vowed he would shoot his bitch that sucked the people's Eggs. I calmly said I never heard of it before and Raleigh Christian was brought to prove that he said so. I examined Raleigh and heard his confidence; on which I put them in mind that not many days ago they were all convinced the curr's resentment had made him say a great deal about Landon bidding [?] him that he afterwards owned was only said out of Spight because he could not beat him. However I asked Selfe about it, he swore it was a lie of Raleigh's, for when he came to tell him Mr. Carter intended to shoot his bitch, he said it was Lawson's bitch and if he had a gun he would shoot her, for she had sucked eggs at his house; and he bad me ask Miss Lucy if, when she spoak to him about his dogs, he did not say he wished they were all killed

This photo of a slave couple in front of their home in Georgia is a rare documentation of slaves' living conditions. Slaves' quarters varied in size and quality according to the number of slaves and their tasks, and were often very close to the master's "big house."

for they were not his, and he did not want them. Lucy owns this, but still to keep up to her female resentment insists he must have said as Raleigh told her brother from an impudent tongue. Alas, how unfit are such good creatures to be judges of anything when once impregnated with resentment.

23. *Wednesday.*

Sukey, the old Granny before spoken of, to be revenged because I would not take her granddaughter away turned out all my Cattle last night on my Cowpen ground which have done me a prodigeous mischief. She has had the impudence to say the child is poor and starved when I declare I never saw a finer, well, fat, nor healthyer child. I will repay this treatment.

**Gabriel's Rebellion, a slave revolt near Richmond, Virginia, in 1800, was one of several ambitious plots of the post–revolutionary era. It was notable for several reasons. First, it was as much urban and coastal as it was rural in character: some of those involved were former slaves or slave artisans—skilled workers who had been hired out to work. These African Americans mingled with working-class whites, and like other seaport workers during this period, they came into contact with the exiles from England, France, Ireland, and the West Indies—people who had left their home countries because of politics or other upheavals of a revolutionary age. The slave rebels took much of their language and inspiration from the American, French, and Haitian revolutions, which they understood to have been about liberty and freedom for ordinary people. Thus they hoped that some native-born whites as well as immigrants would join them in their revolt. Religion also played a crucial role for Gabriel Prosser's followers, who considered their leader to be akin to Moses as well as to George Washington.**

**Thomas Jefferson, the eminent lawyer St. George Tucker, and other white Virginians during this era had been developing schemes for gradual emancipation; some, such as George Washington, freed their slaves in their wills. After the trials and investigations of Gabriel's conspiracy, some Virginians came to believe that the time had arrived to rid Virginia of its slaves, by sending them to the western territories or back to Africa. As the tobacco economy worsened, Virginians continued to get rid of slaves, but instead of shipping them out of the country, they sold them south—to places such as**

Arkansas, Alabama, Tennessee, and Mississippi on the rapidly westward-moving cotton frontier. Newly freed slaves were required to leave Virginia; free blacks came to be seen as threats to the safety of the system. Virginia remained a part of the "solid South" in part because it was the site of several important attacks on the institution of slavery—Gabriel's Rebellion in 1800, the less well known Easter Plot near Petersburg in 1802, Nat Turner's 1831 revolt in Southampton County, and abolitionist John Brown's raid on a federal arsenal at Harpers Ferry in 1859. Such revolts helped convince southerners that slavery could not end gradually: it would end only in war.

The document below is a record of the testimony of Ben Woolfolk at the trial of Gabriel Prosser and the other rebels captured by the authorities.

Sept. 17 [1800]

The first time I ever heard of this conspiricy was from Mrs. Ann Smith's George; the second person that gave me information was Samuel alias Samuel Bird, the property of Mrs. Jane Clarke. They asked me last spring to come over to their houses on a Friday night. It was late before I could get there; the company had met and dispersed. I inquired where they were gone; and was informed to see their wives. I went after them and found George; he carried me and William (the property of William Young) to Sam Bird's, and after we got there he (Sam) enquired of George if he had any pen and ink; he said no—he had left it at home. He brought out his list of men, and he had Elisha Price's Jim, James Price's Moses, Sally Price's Bob, Denny Wood's Emanuel. After this George invited me to come and see him the next night, but I did not go. The following Monday night William went over and returned with a ticket for me; likewise one for Gilbert. The Thursday night following, both George and Sam Bird came to see me. Bowler's Jack was with us. We conversed untill late in the night upon the subject of the meditated war. George said he would try to be ready by the 24th of August, and the following Sunday he went to Hungry meeting-house to enlist men. When I saw him again he informed me he had enlisted 37 men there. The Sunday after he went to Manchester, where he said he had recruited 50-odd men. I never saw him again untill the sermon at my house, which was about three weeks before the rising was to take place. On the day of the sermon, George called on Sam Bird to inform how many men he had; he said he had not his list with him; but he supposed

*Emma Crockett was one of the former slaves interviewed by WPA writers. The WPA interviews are a remarkable record of the everyday lives of slaves in the South and their treatment by their owners.*

### The Risks of Reading

*The Works Progress Administration (WPA), a federal relief program, employed out-of-work scholars and journalists during the depression years of the 1930s. One of their projects was to interview surviving former slaves. They sought to record the former slaves' dialect as they spoke it. Willliam McWhorter was one of those interviewed.*

Lordy, mist'ess, ain't nobody never told you it was agin' de law to larn a nigger to read and write, in slavery time? White folks would chop your hands off for dat quicker dan dey would for'most anything else. Dat's jus' a sayin', "Chop your hands off." Why, mist'ess, a nigger widout no hands wouldn't be able to wuk much, and his owner couldn't sell hem for nigh as much as he could git for a slave wid good hands. Dey jus' beat 'em up bad when dey cotched 'em studyin', readin', or writin', but folks did tell 'bout some of de owners dat cut off one finger evvy time dey cotch a slave tryin' to git larnin'.

How-some-ever, dere was some niggers dat wanted larnin' so bad dey wouls slip out at night and meet in a deep gully what dey would study by de light of lightwood torches. But one thing sho': dey better not let no white folks find out 'bout it, and if dey was lucky nuf' to be able to keep it till day larned to read de Bible, dey kept it a close secret.

about 500. George wished the business to be deferred some time longer. Mr. Prosser's Gabriel wished to bring on the business as soon as possible. Gilbert said the summer was almost over, and he wished them to enter upon the business before the weather got too cold. Gabriel proposed that the subject should be referred to his brother Martin to decide upon. Martin said there was this expression in the Bible, delays breed danger; at this time, he said, the country was at peace, the soldiers were discharged, and the arms all put away; there was no patroling in the country, and that before he would any longer bear what he had borne; he would turn out and fight with his stick. Gilbert said he was ready with his pistol, but it was in need of repair; he gave it to Gabriel, who was put it in order for him. I then spoke to the company and informed them I wished to have something to say. I told them that I had heard in the days of old, when the Israelites were in service to King Pharaoh, they were taken from him by the power of God, and were carried away by Moses. God had blessed him with an angel to go with him, but that I could see nothing of that kind in these days. Martin said in reply: I read in my Bible where God says if we will worship Him we should have peace in all our land; five of you shall conquer an hundred, and a hundred a thousand of our enemies. After this they went on consultation upon the time they should execute the plan. Martin spoke and appointed for them to meet in three weeks, which was to be of a Saturday night. Gabriel said he had 500 bullets made. Smith's George said he was done the corn and would then go on to make as many cross-bows as he could. Bowler's Jack said he had got 50 spiers or bayonets fixed at the ends of sticks. The plan was to be as follows: We were all to meet at the briery spot on the Brook; 100 men were to stand at the Brook bridge; Gabriel was to take 100 more and go to Gregory's tavern and take the arms which were there; 50 more were to be sent to Rocketts to set that on fire, in order to alarm the upper part of the town and induce the people to go down there; while they were employed in extinguishing the fire Gabriel and the other officers and soldiers were to take the Capitol and all the arms they could find and be ready to slaughter the people on their return from Rocketts. Sam Bird was to have a pass as a free man and was to go to the nation of Indians called Catawbas to persuade them to join the negroes to fight the white people. As far as I understood all the whites were to be massacred, except the Quakers, the Methodists, and the Frenchmen, and they were to be spared on account as they conceived of their being friendly to liberty, and also they had understood that the French were at war with this country

*Slave churches such as this one in Goose Creek, South Carolina, were a source of controversy for slave owners. By converting their slaves to Christianity whites dissolved some of the social and cultural distinction between slaves and masters, risked allowing their slaves to become literate, and exposed their slaves to the Christian principles of fellowship and equality among men. Yet as Christians, many owners believed they were obligated to convert their slaves. As a result, whites tried to keep a close watch on black preachers and congregants.*

for the money that was due them, and that an army was landed at South Key, which they hoped would assist them. They intended also to spare all the poor white women who had no slaves.

October 1800

Prosser's Ben—Gabriel was appointed Captain at first consultation respecting the Insurrection, and afterwards when he had enlisted a number of men was appointed General. That they were to kill Mr. Prosser, Mr. Mosby, and all the neighbors, and then proceed to Richmond where they would kill everybody, take the treasury, and divide the money amongst the soldiers; after which he would fortify Richmond and proceed to discipline his men, as [the] apprehended force would be raised elsewhere to repel him. That if the white people agreed to their freedom they would then hoist a white flag, and he would dine and drink with the merchants of the city on the day when it should be agreed to.

Gabriel enlisted a number of negroes. The prisoner went with the witness to Mr. Young's to see Ben Woolfolk, who was going to Caroline to enlist men there. He gave three shillings for himself and three other negroes, to be expended in recruiting men. The prisoner made the handles of the swords, which were made by Solomon. The prisoner shewed the witness a quantity of bullets, nearly a peck, which he and Martin had run, and some lead then on hand, and he said he had ten pounds of powder which he had purchased. Gabriel said he had nearly 10,000 men; he had 1,000 in Richmond, about 600 in Caroline, and nearly 500 at the Coal pits, besides others at different places, and that he expected the poor white people would also join him, and that two Frenchmen had actually joined, whom he said Jack Ditcher knew, but whose names he would not mention to the witness. That the prisoner had enlisted nearly all the negroes in town as he said, and amongst them had 400 Horsemen. That in consequence of the bad weather on Saturday night, an agreement was made to meet at the Tobacco House of Mr. Prosser the ensuing night. Gabriel said all the negroes from Petersburg were to join him after he had commenced the Insurrection.

**A group of slaves in the area of Camden, South Carolina, planned an uprising for the Fourth of July in 1816. They were betrayed by a slave who was eventually rewarded by the South Carolina legislature, which purchased his freedom and gave him a pension of $50 a year for life. The local newspaper lamented that "those who were most active in the conspiracy occupied a respectable stand in the churches." Such events sparked a long-standing debate about whether Christianity made the slaves more contented with their lot or, in fact, made them believe in a spiritual, and real, equality.**

**Rachel Blanding, a New Yorker originally, wrote home to her sister about the rebellion on the day for which it had been planned. The letter was published in a New York newspaper— but when the *Richmond Enquirer* reprinted it, that newspaper left out the sentence in which Blanding refers to the South as a country in which "we cannot go to bed in safety."**

Our village and neighborhood has been in great confusion for two days past owing to the fear of an insurrection of the Blacks. . . . this was the fatal night which was to have accomplished a plan which they have had in agitation since last Christmas, it was their intention to have set fire to one part of town and while the attention of the people was taken up with that they meant to have taken of the Arsenal which is filled with Arms and ammunition and proceeded to murder the men but the women they intended to have reserved for their own purposes this is their own confession. Our Jail is filled with Negroes they are stretched on their backs on the bare floor and scarcely move their heads but have a strong guard placed over them their trials have been going on to day and [six] of the ring leaders are to be executed tomorrow this is really a dreadful situation to be in the Doctor was out on guard last night. I was afraid to sit at home and staid with Sister. I think

### Learning from the Children

*Alice Green was a former slave interviewed by the WPA.*

You'll be s'prised at what Mammy told me 'bout how she got her larnin'. She said she kept a schoolbook hid in her bosom all de time, and when de white chillun got home from school, she would axe 'em lots of questions all 'bout what dey had done larned dat day, and 'cause she was proud of evvy scrap of book larnin' she could pick up, de white chillun larned her how to read, and write, too. All de larnin she ever had she got from de white chillun at de big house, And she was so smart at gittin' 'em to larn her, dat atter de War was over, she got to be a schoolteacher.

it is time for us to leave a Country that we cannot go to bed in safety. Their thirst for revenge must have been great, it was the wish of some to spare some of the whites and they mentioned an Old Gentleman who is a preacher he never owned a Slave and has devoted much of his Time to preaching to them on the plantations but even him they would not spare. I much fear that the execution of those which are now in custody will exasperate the others to do a great deal of mischief. We are indebted to a slave for the discovery of this plan but we shall never know who he is as he requested his master when he told him never to tell his name he said he did not wish to leave this Country and he knew the Negroes would not let him live here the Negroes will never know who betrayed them for they tried to engage all for a good distance round.

**Rachel Blanding wrote to her sister again on July 25, 1816.**

We are much more composed then when I wrote you last in respect of the Negroes there were a great many tried before a respectable court and I believe had every indulgence allowed them that could be under the existing circumstances six of the ringleaders were hung and some others punished two or three confessed the fact and died like heroes they said they were in a good cause one of them who was a professor of religion said he had only one sin to answer for and that was that he had set down to the communion Table with the White people when he knew he was going to cut their Throats as soon as convenient. It has been a most unfortunate event for their survivors they will be treated with more severity than ever. It is the opinion of many that we shall have trouble with them although it is not apprehended at present. The Doctor and myself have determined upon going to the North to live. . . . We have taken such a disgust to Slavery that we cannot feel satisfied here although we are sensible it will be much against our interests to remove.

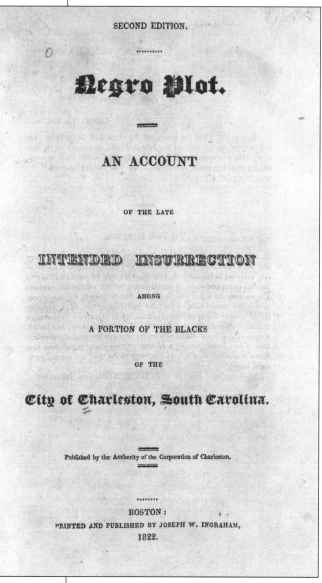

SECOND EDITION.

··········

## Negro Plot.

—

## AN ACCOUNT

OF THE LATE

## INTENDED INSURRECTION

AMONG

A PORTION OF THE BLACKS

OF THE

## City of Charleston, South Carolina.

Published by the Authority of the Corporation of Charleston.

········

BOSTON :
PRINTED AND PUBLISHED BY JOSEPH W. INGRAHAM,
1822.

*This account of the Denmark Vesey rebellion was published by the authority of the Corporation of Charleston, South Carolina, where the rebellion took place. Whites were very interested in the details of slave revolts, hoping to understand the telltale signs of unrest in order to prevent future bloodshed and loss of property.*

**Henry W. DeSaussure, an important planter and politician, lived in Columbia, the capital of South Carolina. He wrote to a friend about the implications of the rebellion and how, as in the case of Gabriel's Rebellion, the attitude and**

## Bloody Consequences

*Denmark Vesey bought his freedom with the proceeds of a winning lottery ticket and went on to plot a major slave uprising in Charleston, South Carolina. This description of Vesey's efforts appeared in* A Narrative of the Conspiracy and Intended Insurrection, Amongst a Portion of the Negroes in the State of South Carolina, In the Year 1822.

He rendered himself perfectly familiar with all those parts of the Scriptures which he thought he could pervert to his purpose, and would readily quote them to prove that slavery was contrary to the laws of God, that slaves were bound to attempt their emancipation, however shocking and bloody might be the consequences, and that such efforts would not only be pleasing to the Almighty, but were absolutely enjoined, and their success predicted in the Scriptures.

**statements of the condemned rebels caused as much unease as the fact of the plot itself.**

We have been alarmed and distressed by accounts from Camden. An Insurrection of the blacks was planned in the neighbouring plantations, a little below [C]amden. Their plan was to rise on the 4th of July & seize the arsenal, & trust to the support of the multitudes who would join them, on the first appearance of success.— A faithful servant of Mr. James Chesnut communicated the plan & the names of the ringleaders to him. . . .

[T]hey met death with the heroism of Spartans, & displayed a Spirit worthy of a better Cause. . . . They pleaded guilty, & glories in their plan. This is an awful thing. There is indeed no danger to the Country, even in case of a first successful attempt, but many families might be butchered, & useful lives lost.—The tone, & temper of these leaders is alarming, or it was of a cast not suited, to their condition—and showed they have imbibed deeply the principles of liberty, & a contempt of death in pursuit of it. And this is the most dangerous state of mind for slaves. Doubtless the detection & punishment of the leaders, will repress it for a time—but I fear the Spirit has sunk too deep in the minds of these people.

## Disobedience and Discipline

**This 1847 letter of George Skipwith, a plantation overseer in Alabama, to his employer describes the frequent mediation that occurred between field slaves and their masters. Overseers such as Skipwith reminded masters of the potential threat of such a largely unsupervised group. Owners and overseers severely punished breaches of discipline that occurred in front of other slaves because of the potential of such actions to inspire others.**

Sir                              hopewell July the 8 1847
on the forth day of July i reseved your letter dated may the 25. i wrote to you the 15 of June the second time giveing you a true statement of the crops, horses, hogs, and chickens. but i am sorry that I shall have to [write] you princeable about other matters. I hav a good crop on hand for you, borth of cotten and corn. this you know could not be don without hard work. i have worked the people but not out of reason. and i have whiped none without caus  the persons whome i have correct i will tell you thir name and thir faults. Suky who I put to plant som corn and after she had

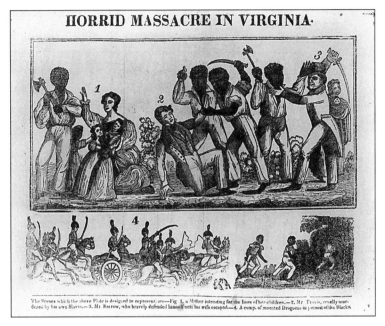

HORRID MASSACRE IN VIRGINIA.

The Scenes which the above Plate is designed to represent, are—Fig. 1, a Mother intreating for the lives of her children.—2. Mr. Travis, cruelly murdered by his own Slaves.—3. Mr. Barrow, who bravely defended himself until his wife escaped.—4. A comp. of mounted Dragoons in pursuit of the Blacks.

been ther long anuf to have been done i went there and she had hardly began it    i gave her some four or five licks over her clothes i gave isham too licks over his clothes for coveering up cotten with the plow. I put frank, isham, Evally, Dinah, Jinny evealine and Charlott to sweeping cotten going twice in a roe. and at a Reasonable days worke they ought to hav plowed seven accers a peice. and they had been at it a half of a day. and they had not done more than one accer and a half and i gave them ten licks a peace upon their skins    i gave Evlyann eight or ten licks for misplacing her hoe. that was all the whiping I hav done from the time that I pitched the crop untell we commenced cutting oats. I put Shadrack, Robert, Armstead, and frank to cutting. they commence on friday, but they did not more than urn the Salt in thir bread. but the next morning i went out there and staid untill a late breakfast, and i saw that the lick that they had then. they were about to do a pretty good days worke. i then leave them and went to the hoe hands, marking the last roe they cut while i was there. when i come to them at twelve o clocke, they had cut some nineteen roes. and it would not take them more than ten minutes to cut one roe. as Shadrack was the ruler among them, i spoke these words to him, you do not intend to cut these oats untill i whip every one of you. Shadrack did not say any thing to me. but Robert spoke these words saying that he knoed when he worked. i told him to shut his lips and if he spoke a nother worde i would whip him right of[f] but he spoke again the second time saying that he was not afraid of being whiped by no man. i then gave him a cut with

**The Cause of Liberty**

*William Lloyd Garrison wrote a preface to Douglass's* Narrative. *In it Garrison describes his reaction the first time Douglass spoke about his experiences before an audience.*

As soon as he had taken his seat, filled with hope and admiration, I rose, and declared that PATRICK HENRY, of revolutionary fame, never made a speech more eloquent in the cause of liberty.

*This scene of an overseer at work painted by Benjamin Henry Latrobe, an American architect sympathetic to the antislavery cause, illustrates the cruel inequities of slavery. The man stands idly smoking while the two slave women hoe the ground.*

the whip. he then flong down his cradle and made a oath and said that he had as li[k]e die as to live and he said that he did not intend to stay here. he then tried to take the whip out of my hand, but i caught him fast by the collar and holed him. i then told the other boys to strip him and they don so     i then whiped untell i thought that he was pretty could but i was deseived for as soon as i leave him and went to the hoe hands, he come up to the house to our preacher and his family becaus he knoed that they would protect him in his Rascality for he had herd that they had said that they were worked to death and that they were lowed no more chance for liveing than they were dogs or hogs. tho the preacher did not say any thing to me about whiping Robert neither to mas John but went down to the Shop and holed about an hours chat with the negroes     i do not knoe what his chat was to them but i ask Dr.Weeb. what was good for a negro that w[as] whipt albut to death and he had much to say about it. Dr. Weeb saw that his chat was calculated to incurage the people to rebel against me, and he went and told mas John about what he had herd and mas John took him and come up here to see if he was punished in the way he had herd. but as soon as the Dr put his hand upon him he told mas John that there was nothing the matter with him. mas John then ordered him to his worke and told him that he did not have what his crime was deserving him, and at some lesure time he intend to give him a good wallening and then he would knoe how to behave him self. he rode over the land and saw what they had done, and instead of finding fault of me he said i ought to have given the other three the same. I have not room to write you as I would wish. I will inform you in my next letter what fencing i have done then you can Judge whither i had any time or not. i have a nuf yet to write you to fill up another sheat. permit me to say a few words to you in James letter. we have our family worship every morning  Beleave me to be your Servant
    George Skipwith

**Besides being whipped (a punishment often administered in front of other slaves), disobedient slaves could be sold**

further south—perhaps all the way to Cuba, where conditions were generally known to be harsher and where slaves would probably never see their friends and family again. In this 1861 letter from an overseer on a Chatham County, Georgia, plantation, the slaves seem to have resisted being taken from one plantation to another and were threatened with being sold to yet another for their resistance.

Dear Sir: At 9 3/4 Ocl., reached here all Negroes doing well, the three are safe, Big George, Dov. Jack, Little George. Ishomail begged to remain; he betrayed his brother and little George. Jack caught in Back River by Driver John, in the small canoe; he resisted the Driver. George (big) attempted to run off in presen[ce] of the entire force and in my presen[ce]. He was caught by Driver John between Conveyor House and No. 1 door. I gave him 60 straps in presen[ce] of those he ran off in presen[ce] of. Everything else is as quiet as possible. Gentlemen be assured I will act in a calm and determined manner; I will stand by your interests until there is no more of me. I apprehend but little trouble after a week or so. The three men should be sent away, and if you can obtain $1000, for big George "to be sent to Cuba" let him go or you will loose him; he should not be among a gang of Negroes. I have not time or space to write all.

Within the institution of southern slavery, slaves succeeded in creating their own lives, apart from the oversight of the master. The demand for cheap labor was such that whites

Miss Fillis and child, and Bill, Sold at publick Sale in May 12th. Christiansburg, montgomery County.

Lewis Miller, a traveler from Pennsylvania, sketched this auction scene in his journal around 1853. While some slaves remained on the same plantation from birth to death, others were sold from owner to owner and moved from state to state throughout their lives, losing all contact with their families and former homes.

## Toil Without Thought

*Slave owners often saw themselves as good providers for their slaves and insisted that slaves had happy lives. Lengthy toil, masters convinced themselves, was good for blacks. A Mississippi planter wrote in a short essay for the southern magazine* DeBow's Review, *in 1851:*

It is a fact established beyond all controversy, that when the negro is treated with humanity, and subjected to constant employment without the labor of thought, and the cares incident to the necessity of providing for his own support, he is by far happier than he would be if emancipated, and left to think, and act, and provide for himself.

who could not afford slaves might hire other people's slaves on the side. Using the gardens they were given for growing their own food, slaves also raised vegetables or other products for the market. This advertisement, published on August 9, 1819, in the *Town Gazette & Farmer's Register* of Clarksville, Tennessee, reveals one master's frustration with such independence.

NOTICE. Whereas my negroes have been much in the habit of working at night for such persons as will employ them, to the great injury of their health and morals. I therefore forbid all persons employing them without my special permission in writing. I also forbid trading with them, buying from or selling to them, without my written permit stating the article they may buy or sell. The law will be strictly enforced against transgressors, without respect to persons.

MORGAN BROWN.

# Subversion, Suffering, and Escape

Which view of slaves was the true one? Masters saw either happy obedience or dangerous opposition, but most of the time relations were somewhere in between. The culture of slavery—its everyday rules, its possibilities for expression and action—required slaves to be very careful in what they said or did. Some slaves became experts in the art of saying, or seeming to say, one thing and meaning something different, even opposite. For this reason, scholars have called attention to the extraordinary amount of acting that had become basic to the system of American slavery by the 19th century. Whether thought of as "masks," a "charade," or even a ritual, relations between slaves and masters involved calculated pretense and subterfuge. In *The Narrative of Lunsford Lane, Formerly of Raleigh, North Carolina* (1848), the fugitive slave Lunsford Lane explained that he would have been in grave danger had he ever revealed what he was really thinking.

Ever after I entertained the first idea of being free, I had endeavored so to conduct myself as not to become obnoxious to the white inhabitants, knowing as I did their power, and their hostility to the colored people. The two points necessary in such a case I had kept constantly in mind. First, I made no display of the little property or money I possessed, but in every way I wore as much as possible the aspect of slavery. Second, I had never appeared to be even so intelligent as I really was. This all colored people at the south, free and slaves, find it peculiarly necessary for their own comfort and safety to observe.

**Such pretense on the part of blacks allowed for a great deal of everyday resistance through humor. Indeed, one of the stereotypes of southern slaves has always been that they had good senses of humor; masters sometimes ordered their slaves to perform for them, unaware (perhaps) that the slaves' jokes and powers of mimicry were used to make fun of the masters once their backs were turned. White northerners turned this kind of humor—in which the joke is often on the more powerful person, who assumes that the person he is talking to is stupid, lying, or both—into the mainstay of the minstrel show, one of the most popular forms of entertainment in 19th-century cities. A good example is this joke, in the form of a conversation between a slave named Pompey and his master.**

African-American music, as reinterpreted by whites in minstrel shows, was reproduced in songbooks such as Plantation Melodies. *The depiction of the musicians as childlike and happy is typical of some popular representations of slaves during the 19th century.*

Pompey, how do I look?
O, massa, mighty.
What do you mean, "mighty," Pompey?
Why, massa, you look noble.
What do you mean by "noble"?
Why, sar, you look just like one lion.
Why, Pompey, where have you ever seen a lion?
I see one down in yonder field the other day, massa.
Pompey, you foolish fellow, that was a jackass.
Was it, massa? Well you look just like him.

**For some slaves, a particular kind of knowledge—the ability to read and write—provided a path to freedom. At the heart of Frederick Douglass's powerful *Narrative* of his life as a slave is the transformation he achieved through learning how to read—and the threat reading represented to the masters, even though some believed it was only right to teach slaves to read. For Douglass and other abolitionists, as for David Walker two decades earlier, part of the cause of slaves' suffering was their "ignorance": slavery was a system of mental as well as physical oppression. Because reading was the symbol of substance in this era of proliferating**

**newspapers and books, the ability to read served Douglass as both a symbol of wisdom and a tool of emancipation. Douglass also aimed his life story at white northerners, arguing that the South was itself becoming a land of ignorance because it taught masters and mistresses to be inhumane. Ultimately, according to Douglass, he *stole* literacy from whites, much as he had to steal himself from their legal possession.**

Very soon after I went to live with Mr. and Mrs. Auld, she very kindly commenced to teach me the A, B, C. After I had learned this, she assisted me in learning to spell words of three or four letters. Just at this point of my progress, Mr. Auld found out what was going on, and at once forbade Mrs. Auld to instruct me further, telling her, among other things, that it was unlawful, as well as unsafe, to teach a slave to read. To use his own words, further, he said, "If you give a nigger an inch, he will take an ell. A nigger should know nothing but to obey his master—to do as he is told to do. Learning would spoil the best nigger in the world. NOW," said he, "if you teach that nigger (speaking of myself) how to read, there would be no keeping him. It would forever unfit him to be a slave. He would at once become unmanageable, and of no value to his master. As to himself, it could do him no good, but a great deal of harm. It would make him discontented and unhappy." These words sank deep into my heart, stirred up sentiments within that lay slumbering, and called into existence an entirely new train of thought. It was a new and special revelation, explaining dark and mysterious things, with which my youthful understanding had struggled, but struggled in vain. I now understood what had been to one a most perplexing difficulty—to wit, the white man's power to enslave the black man. It was a grand achievement, and I prized it highly. From that moment, I understood the pathway from slavery to freedom. It was just what I wanted, and I got it at a time when I the least expected it. Whilst I was saddened by the thought of losing the aid of my kind mistress, I was gladdened by the invaluable instruction which, by the merest accident, I had gained from my master. Though conscious of the difficulty of learning without a teacher, I set out with high hope, and a fixed purpose, at whatever cost of trouble, to learn how to read.

In accomplishing this, I was compelled to resort to various stratagems. I had no regular teacher. My mistress, who had kindly commenced to instruct me, had, in compliance with the advice and direction of her husband, not only ceased to instruct, but had set her face against my being instructed by any one else. It is due, however, to my mistress to say of her, that she did not adopt this course of treatment immediately. She at first lacked the depravity indispensable to shutting me up in mental darkness. It was at least necessary for her to have some training in the exercise of irresponsible power, to make her equal to the task of treating me though I were a brute.

My mistress was, as I have said, a kind and tender-hearted woman; and in the simplicity of her soul she commenced, when I first went to live with her, to treat me as she supposed one human being ought to treat another. In entering upon the duties of a slaveholder, she did not seem to perceive that I sustained to her the relation of a mere chattel, and that for her to treat me as a human being was not only wrong, but dangerously so. Slavery proved as injurious to her as it did to me. When I went there, she was a pious, warm, and tender-hearted woman. There was no sorrow or suffering for which she had not a tear. She had bread for the hungry, clothes for the naked, and comfort for every mourner that came within her reach. Slavery soon proved its ability to divest her of these heavenly qualities. Under its influence, the tender heart became stone, and the lamblike disposition gave way to one of tiger-like fierceness. The first step in her downward course was in her ceasing to instruct me. She now commenced to practice her husband's precepts. She finally became even more violent in her opposition than her husband himself. She was not satisfied with simply doing as well as he has commanded; she seemed anxious to do better. Nothing seemed to make her more angry than to see me with a newspaper. She seemed to think that here lay the danger. I have had her rush at me with a face made all up of fury, and snatch from me a newspaper, in a manner that fully revealed her apprehension. She was an apt woman; and a little experience soon demonstrated, to her satisfaction, that education and slavery were incompatible with each other.

One argument used to justify slavery was that slaves' labor kept them "balanced" and that they would not know how to "walk for themselves" if granted their freedom. This idea that slaves were unable to care or think for themselves was also used as an excuse to keep slaves illiterate.

From this time I was most narrowly watched. If I was in a separate room any considerable length of time, I was sure to be suspected of having a book, and was at once called to give account of myself. All this, however, was too late. The first step had been taken. Mistress, in teaching me the alphabet, had given me the inch, and no precaution could prevent me from taking the ell.

The plan which I adopted, and the one by which I was most successful, was that of making friends of all the little white boys whom I met in the street. As many of these as I could, I converted into teachers. With their kindly aid, obtained at different times and in different places, I finally succeeded in learning to read. When I was sent of errands, I always took my book with me, and by going one part of my errand quickly, I found time to get a lesson before my return. I used also to carry bread with me, enough of which was always in the house, and to which I was always welcome; for I was much better off in this regard than many of the poor white children in our neighborhood. This bread I used to bestow upon the hungry little urchins, who, in return, would give me that more valuable bread of knowledge. I am strongly tempted to give the names of two or three of those little boys, as a testimonial of the gratitude and affection I bear them; but prudence forbids;—not that it would injure me, but it might embarrass them; for it is almost an unpardonable offense to teach slaves to read in this Christian country. It is enough to say of the dear little fellows, that they lived on Philpot Street, very near Durgin and Bailey's ship-yard. I used to talk this matter of slavery over with them. I would sometimes say to them, I wished I could be free as they would be when they got to be men. "You will be free as soon as you are twenty-one, *but I am a slave for life!* Have not I as good a right to be free as you have?" These words used to trouble them; they would express for me the liveliest sympathy, and console me with the hope that something would occur by which I might be free.

I was now about twelve years old, and the thought of being *a slave for life* began to bear heavily upon my heart. Just about this time, I got hold of a book entitled "The Columbian Orator." Every opportunity I got, I used to read this book. Among much of other interesting matter, I found in it a dialogue between a master and his slave. The slave was represented as having run away from his master three times. The dialogue represented the conversation which took place between them, when the slave was retaken the third time. In this dialogue, the whole argument in behalf of slavery was brought forward by the master, all of which was disposed of by the slave. The slave was made to say some very smart as well as impressive things in reply to his master—things which had the desired though unexpected effect; for the conversation resulted in the voluntary emancipation of the slave on the part of the master.

In the same book, I met with one of Sheridan's mighty speeches on and in behalf of Catholic emancipation. These were choice documents to me. I read them over and over again with unabated interest. They gave tongue to interesting thoughts of my own soul, which had frequently flashed through my mind, and died away for want of utterance. The moral which I gained form the dialogue was the power of truth over conscience of even a slaveholder. What I got from Sheridan was a bold denunciation of slavery, and a powerful vindication of human rights. The readings of these documents enabled me to utter my thoughts, and to meet the arguments brought forward to sustain slavery; but while they relieved me to of one difficulty, they brought on another even more painful than the one of which I was relieved. The more I read, the more I was led to abhor and detest my enslavers. I could regard them in no other light than a band of successful robbers, who had left their homes, and gone to Africa, and stolen us from our homes, and in a strange land reduced us to slavery. I loathed them as being the meanest as well as the most wicked of men. As I read and contemplated the subject, behold! that very discontentment which Master Hugh had predicted would follow my learning to read had already come, to torment and sting my soul to unutterable anguish. As I writhed under it, I would at times feel that learning to read had been a curse rather than a blessing. It had given me a view of my wretched condition, without the remedy. It opened my eyes to the horrible pit, but to no ladder upon which to get out. In moments of agony, I envied my fellow-slaves for their stupidity. I have often wished myself a beast. I preferred the condition of the meanest reptile to my own. Any thing, no matter

*In her will, Margaret Horniblow bequeaths her slave girl, Harriet Jacobs, to her niece along with some furniture. Even the death of a slave's owner did not bring freedom to the slave. Bondage was handed down through the generations and slaves could be inherited or traded like any other form of property.*

ONE HUNDRED DOLLARS REWARD—Ran away from the subscriber, living in Port Gibson, Miss., on the 15th of March last, a mulatto slave, aged about 16 years, named HARRY, sometimes called ZIP, a good looking boy and well grown for his age: no scars remembered except a cut on the first toe of the right foot, which causes the toe to turn down; when spoken to is much in the habit of casting his eyes to the ground. I will give $50 for the apprehension and delivery of said boy to me, in Port Gibson, if taken in the State of Mississippi; and if taken, out of the State, $100. It is very probable said boy may have a pass or free papers—if so, they are not genuine. He has a fine head of hair, not kinky, but black and wavy. He will perhaps endeavor to make his way to some free State.
SAMUEL MARTIN.
Port Gibson, April 25, 1856.            ap29—1m ¶

TWENTY-FIVE DOLLARS REWARD—Ran away from Richland Plantation, near New Carthage, parish of Madison, La., on the 4th inst., the black boy EDWARD, belonging to the estate of Robert Dunbar. The said Edward is about 18 years old, about 5 feet 6 inches tall. The above reward will be paid for his apprehension and lodging in jail, or delivery to the overseer on plantation. Address agent of said estate at Natchez, Miss., or
GEO. CONNELLY, 43 Carondelet street,
ap9—1m                                    New Orleans

REWARD—One Hundred and Twenty-Five Dollars Reward for the apprehension of the griff boy named DANIEL, aged about 12 years; has weak or inflamed eyes, and thick lips; had on a blue check shirt and cloth pantaloons; left his owner's domicil on Sunday morning, 27th inst. The above reward will be paid for the proof, to conviction, of the party or parties who have the said boy harbored, or twenty-five dollars for his delivery to the subscriber. It is verily believed that the boy has been kidnapped for the purpose of taking him out of the State, as he was purchased from a trader from Mobile. All masters of steamboats are hereby cautioned against taking said boy away, as they will be prosecuted accordingly.
ap28—5t ¶           THOMAS FELLOWS, 7 Camp street.

TWENTY DOLLARS REWARD  For arresting the slave HENRIETTA, a griffe girl, aged about thirty years; has a mark upon her arm from a burn; walks very quick; was heard of last March, 29th, hunting for a master; was last on Duplantier street; speaks English alone.  The above reward will be paid upon her being lodged in jail, and information left at the lumber yard, Common street, No. 247, or Gasquet street, No. 14, between Canal and Common.
ap19—tf ¶

ONE HUNDRED AND FIFTY DOLLARS REWARD—Ran away on the night of the 19th February, the mulatto girl MARY MACKENDISH, aged about 32 years, of small stature, round face, long hair, and not curled; her upper teeth are out.  The above reward will be paid to any person who will lodge her in the city jail, or deliver her at No. 64 Toulouse street, corner of Royal.
☞ Captains of steamboats are hereby cautioned not to receive said girl on board, as it is supposed that she will try to go up the river.                           ap20—1m

TWENTY-FIVE DOLLARS REWARD—Ran away from the subscribers, the griff boy WILLIAM, a native of the city, pockmarked, aged about 36 years, a well known hack driver, speaks French and English. He is probably lurking about the city.  The above reward will be paid to any person lodging him in jail and returning him to us.
H. M. ROBINSON & CO.,
ap24—tf ¶                      100 Gravier street.

TWENTY DOLLARS REWARD—Ran away from the subscriber, the boy TOM.  Said boy is black, 5 feet 7 or 8 inches high, has a piece out of one ear, is about 26 years old.  The above reward will be paid if he is lodged in any jail in the State; if caught in a free State, I will pay $500 if he is brought to me in New Orleans.          JOHN ERMON.

*Running away was an important path to freedom. This list of advertisements for runaways printed in the New Orleans* Daily Picayune *is an indication of the fairly constant trickle of slaves away from the plantations that helped erode slavery's hold on the South.*

what to get rid of thinking! It was this everlasting thinking of my condition that tormented me. There was no getting rid of it. It was pressed upon me by every object within sight or hearing, animate or inanimate. The silver trump of freedom had roused my soul to eternal wakefulness. Freedom now appeared, to disappear, no more forever. It was heard in every sound, and seen in every thing. It was ever present to torment me with a sense of my wretched condition. I saw nothing without seeing it, I heard nothing without hearing it, and felt nothing without feeling it. It looked from every star, it smiled in every calm, breathed in every wind, and moved in every storm.

I often found myself regretting my own existence, and wishing myself dead; and but for the hope of being free, I have no doubt but that I should have killed myself, or done something for which I should have been killed. While in this state of mind, I was eager to hear any one speak of slavery. I was a ready listener. Every little while, I could hear something about the abolitionists. It was some time before I found what the word meant. It was always used in such connections as to make it an interesting word to me. If a slave ran away and succeeded in getting clear, or if a slave killed his master, set fire to the barn, or did any thing very wrong in the mind of a slaveholder, it was spoken of as the fruit of abolition. Hearing the word in this connection very often, I set about learning what it meant. The dictionary afforded me little or no help. I found it was "the act of abolishing," but then I did not know what was to be abolished. Here I was perplexed. I did not dare to ask any one about its meaning, for I was satisfied that it was something they wanted me to know very little about. After a patient waiting, I got one of our city papers, containing an account of the number of petitions from the north, praying for the abolition of slavery in the District of Columbia, and of the slave trade between the States. From this time I understood the words *abolition* and *abolitionist,* and always drew near when that word was spoken, expecting to hear something of importance to myself and fellow-slaves. The light broke in upon me by degrees. I went one day down on the wharf of Mr. Waters; and seeing two Irishmen unloading a scow of stone, I went, unasked, and helped them. When we had finished, one of them came to me and asked me if I was a slave. I told him I was. The good Irishman seemed to be deeply affected by the statement. He said to the other that it was a pity so fine a little fellow as myself should be a slave for life. He said it was a shame to hold me. They both advised me to run away to the north; that I should find friends there, and that I should be free. I pretended not to be interested in what they said, and treated them as if I did not understand them for I feared they might be treacherous. White men have been known to encourage slaves to escape, and then, to get the reward, catch them, and return them to their masters. I was afraid that these seemingly good men ought use me so; but I nevertheless remembered their advice, and from that time I resolved to run away. I looked forward to a time at which it would be safe for me to escape. I was too young to think of doing so immediately; besides, I wished to learn how to write, as I might have occasion to write my own pass. I consoled myself with the hope that I should one day find a good chance. Meanwhile, I would learn to write.

The idea as to how I might learn to write was suggested to me by being in Durgin and Bailey's ship-yard, and frequently seeing the ship carpenters, after hewing, and getting a piece of timber ready for use, write on the timber the name of that part of the ship for which it was intended. When a piece of timber was intended for the larboard side, it would be marked thus—"L." When a piece was for the starboard side, it would be marked this—"S." A piece for the larboard side forward, would be marked this—"L.F." When a piece was for the starboard aft, it would be marked thus—"S.A." I soon learned the names of these letters, and for what they were intended when placed upon a piece of timber in the ship-yard. I immediately commenced copying them, and in a short time was able to make the four letters named. After that, when I met with any boy who I knew could write, I would tell him I could write as well as he. The next word would be, "I don't believe you. Let me see you try it." I would then make the letters which I had been so fortunate as to learn, and ask him to beat that. In this way I got a good many lessons in writing, which it is quite possible I should never have gotten in any other way. During this time, my copy-book was the board fence, brick wall, and the pavement; and my pen and ink was a lump of chalk. With these, I learned mainly how to write. I then commenced and continued copying the Italics in Webster's Spelling Book, until I could make them all without looking at the book. By this time, my little Master Thomas had gone to school, and learned how to write, and had written over a number of copybooks. These had been brought home, and shown to some of our near neighbors, and then laid aside. My mistress used to go to class meeting every Monday afternoon, and leave me to take care of the house. When left thus, I used to spend time in writing in the spaces left in Master Thomas's copy-book, copying what he had written. I continued to do this until I could write very similar to that of Master Thomas. Thus, after a long, tedious effort for years, I finally succeeded in learning how to write.

**Another important theme in the life of southern slaves' lives, and one that spurred many acts of resistance, was the ruination of slave families. Masters not only sold away slave children but also sometimes seduced or even raped female slaves. Harriet Jacobs hid from her master out of fear. Writing for a northern white audience about the horrors of slavery, in her _Incidents in the Life of a Slave Girl, Written by Herself_ (1861), Jacobs argued that slaves wanted to have close family relations, including marriages, like free people, but their situation made such a family life nearly impossible. As a result, she said, they should not be judged immoral, according to the standards of the day. For abolitionists, the assaults that occurred within the plantation household proved that the entire slave system was immoral. In their published narratives and lectures, former slaves turned their personal histories into potent political weapons against slavery.**

During the first years of my service in Dr. Flint's family, I was accustomed to share some indulgences with the children of my mistress. Though this seemed to me no more than right, I was grateful for it, and tried to merit the kindness by the faithful discharge of my duties. But I now entered on my fifteenth year—a sad epoch in the life of a slave girl. My master began to whisper foul words in my ear. Young as I was, I could not remain ignorant of their import. I tried to treat them with indifference or contempt. The master's age, my extreme youth, and the fear that his conduct would be reported to my grandmother, made him bear this treatment for many months. He was a crafty man, and resorted to many means to accomplish his purposes. Sometimes he had stormy, terrific ways, that made his victims tremble; sometimes he assumed a gentleness that he thought must surely subdue. Of the two, I preferred his stormy moods, although they left me trembling. He tried his utmost to corrupt the pure principles my grandmother had instilled. He peopled my young mind with unclean images, such as only a vile monster could think of. I turned from him with disgust and hatred. But he was my master. I was compelled to live under the same roof with him—where I saw a man forty years my senior daily violating the most sacred commandments of nature. He told me I was his property; that I must be subject to his will in all things. My soul revolted against the mean tyranny. But where could I turn for protection? No matter whether the slave girl be as black as ebony or as fair as her mistress. In either case, there is no shadow of law to protect her from insult, from violence, or even from death; all these are inflicted by fiends who bear the shape of men. The mistress, who ought to protect the helpless victim, has no other feelings towards her but those of jealousy and rage. The degradation, the wrongs, the vices, that grow out of slavery, are more than I can describe. They are greater than you would willingly believe. Surely, if you credited one half the truths that are told you concerning the helpless millions suffering in this cruel bondage, you at the north would not help to tighten the yoke. You surely would refuse to do for the master, on your own soil, the mean and cruel work which trained bloodhounds and the lowest class of whites do for him at the south.

Every where the years bring to all enough of sin and sorrow; but in slavery the very dawn of life is darkened by these shadows. Even the little child, who is accustomed to wait on her mistress and her children, will learn, before she is twelve years old, why it is that her mistress hates such and such a one among the slaves. Perhaps the child's own mother is among those hated ones. She listens to violent outbreaks of jealous passion, and cannot help understanding what is the cause. She will become prematurely knowing in evil things. Soon she will learn to tremble when she hears her master's footfall. She will be compelled to realize that she is no longer a child. If God has bestowed beauty upon her, it will prove her greatest curse. That which commands admiration in the white woman only hastens the degradation of the female slave. I know that some are too much brutalized by slavery to feel the humiliation of their position; but many slaves feel it most acutely, and shrink from the memory of it. I cannot tell how much I suffered in the presence of these wrongs, nor how I am still pained by the retrospect. My master met me at every turn, reminding me that I belonged to him, and swearing by heaven and earth that he would compel me to submit to him. If I went out for a breath of fresh air, after a day of unwearied toil, his footsteps dogged me. If I knelt by my mother's grave, his dark shadow fell on me even there. The light heart which nature had given me became heavy and sad forebodings. The other slaves in my master's house noticed the change. Ma[n]y of them pitied me; but none dared to ask the cause. They had no need to inquire. They

Believed to be a toy made for a slave's child, this doll was found in a plantation attic in North Carolina. Even though they could be sold and forever separated, slaves formed families and were attached to their children.

knew too well the guilty practices under that roof; and they were aware that to speak of them was an offence that never went unpunished.

**In the intervening chapters, Mrs. Flint responds angrily to Dr. Flint's treatment of the young slave, and Jacobs seeks the love and protection of a free black man. After Jacob's lover tries, unsuccessfully, to buy her from Dr. Flint so he can marry her, he leaves for the North.**

After my lover went away, Dr. Flint contrived a new plan. He seemed to have an idea that my fear of my mistress was his greatest obstacle. In the blandest tones, he told me that he was going to build a small house for me, in a secluded place, four miles away from the town. I shuddered; but I was constrained to listen, while he talked of his intention to give me a home of my own, and to make a lady of me. Hitherto, I had escaped my dreaded fate, by being in the midst of people. My grandmother had already had high words with my master about me. She had told him pretty plainly what she thought of his character, and there was considerable gossip in the neighborhood about our affairs, to which the open-mouthed jealousy of Mrs. Flint contributed not a little. When my master said he was going to build a house for me, and that he could do it with little trouble and expense, I was in hopes something would happen to frustrate his scheme; but I soon heard that the house was actually begun. I vowed before my Maker that I would never enter it. I had rather toil on the plantation from dawn till dark; I had rather live and die in jail, than drag on, from day to day, through such a living death. I was determined that the master, whom I so hated and loathed, who had blighted the prospects of my youth, and made my life a desert, should not, after my long struggle with him, succeed at last in trampling his victim under his feet. I would do any thing, every thing, for the sake of defeating him. What *could* I do? I thought and thought, till I became desperate, and made a plunge into the abyss.

And now, reader, I come to a period in my unhappy life, which I would gladly forget if I could. The remembrance fills me with sorrow and shame. It pains me to tell you of it; but I have promised to tell you the truth, and I will do it honestly, let it cost me what it may. I will not try to screen myself behind the plea of compulsion from a master; for it was not so. Neither can I plead ignorance or thoughtlessness. For years, my master had done his utmost to pollute my mind with foul images, and to destroy the pure principles inculcated by my grandmother, and the good mistress of my childhood. The influences of slavery had had the same effect on me that they had on other young girls; they made me prematurely knowing, concerning the evil ways of the world. I knew what I did, and I did it with deliberate calculation.

But, O, ye happy women, whose purity has been sheltered from childhood, who have been free to choose the objects of your affection, whose homes are protected by law, do not judge the poor desolate slave girl too severely! If slavery had been abolished, I, also, could have married the man of my choice; I could have had a home shielded by the laws; and I should have been spared the painful task of confessing what I am now about to relate; but all my prospects had been blighted by slavery. I wanted to keep myself pure; and, under the most adverse circumstances, I tried hard to preserve my self-respect; but I was struggling alone in the powerful grasp of the demon Slavery; and the monster proved too strong for me. I felt as if I was forsaken by God and man; as if all my efforts must be frustrated; and I became reckless in my despair.

I have told you that Dr. Flint's persecutions and his wife's jealousy had give rise to some gossip in the neighborhood. Among others, it chanced that a white unmarried gentleman had obtained some knowledge of the circumstances in which I was placed. He knew my grandmother, and often spoke to me in the street. He became interested for me, and asked questions about my master, which I answered in part. He expressed a great deal of sympathy, and a wish to aid me. He constantly sought opportunities to see me, and wrote to me frequently. I was a poor slave girl, only fifteen years old.

So much attention from a superior person was, of course, flattering; for human nature is the same in all. I also felt grateful for his sympathy, and encouraged by his kind words. It seemed to me a great thing to have such a friend. By degrees, a more tender feeling crept into my heart. He was an educated and eloquent gentleman;

This depiction of the "luxuries" of white Virginians—the sexual pleasures they took from female slaves and the whipping they gave to male slaves—was painted on the back panel of a formal portrait of an unknown man. Much like this hidden painting, women slaves' lack of even sexual freedom from their masters was an unspoken truth behind the institution of slavery.

too eloquent, alas, for the poor slave girl who trusted in him. Of course I saw whither all this was tending. I knew the impassable gulf between us; but to be an object of interest to a man who is not married, and who is not her master, is agreeable to the pride and feelings of a slave, if her miserable situation has left her any pride or sentiment. It seems less degrading to give one's self, than to submit to compulsion. There is something akin to freedom in having a lover who has no control over you, except that which he gains by kindness and attachment. A master may treat you as rudely as he pleases, and you dare not speak; moreover, the wrong does not seem so great with an unmarried man, as with one who has a wife to be made unhappy. There may be sophistry in all this; but the condition of a slave confuses all principles of morality, and, in fact, renders the practice of them impossible.

When I found that my master had actually begun to build the lonely cottage, other feelings mixed with those I have described. Revenge, and calculations of interest, were added to flattered vanity and sincere gratitude for kindness. I knew nothing would enrage Dr. Flint so much as to know that I favored another; and it was something to triumph over my tyrant even in that small way. I thought he would revenge himself by selling me, and I was sure my friend, Mr. Sands, would buy me. He was a man of more generosity and feeling than 'my master, and I thought my freedom could be easily obtained from him. The crisis of my fate now came so near that I was desperate. I shuddered to think of being the mother of children that should be owned by my old tyrant. I knew that as soon as a new fancy took him, his victims were sold far off to get rid of them; especially if they had children. I had seen several women sold, with his babies at the breast. He never allowed his offspring by slaves to remain long in sight of himself and his wife. Of a man who was not my master I could ask to have my children well supported; and in this case, I felt confident I should obtain the boon. I also felt quite sure that they would be made free. With all these thoughts revolving in my mind, and seeing no other way of escaping the doom, I so much dreaded, I made a headlong plunge. Pity me, and pardon me, O virtuous reader! You never knew what it is to be a slave; to be entirely unprotected by law or custom; to have the laws reduce you to the condition of a chattel, entirely subject to the will of another. You never exhausted your ingenuity in avoiding the snares, and eluding the power of a hated tyrant; you never shuddered at the sound of his footsteps, and trembled within hearing of his voice. I know I did wrong. No one can feel it more sensibly than I do. The painful and humiliating memory will haunt me to my dying day. Still, in looking back, calmly, on the events of my life, I feel that the slave woman ought not to be judged by the same standard as others.

**One of the most famous fugitive slaves was Henry ("Box") Brown. Brown's story of packing himself into a crate and sending the package north by U.S. mail was told again and again because it illustrated the intelligence and creativity of African Americans. In his *History of the Underground Railroad* (1872), William Still, one of the chief "conductors" of the Underground Railroad, wrote memorably of the moment when Brown first arrived in Philadelphia, on a very real train, at the end of his last journey as an article of property. Upon emerging from his box and asking, "How do you do, gentlemen?" Brown claimed his new status as an equal, even as another "gentleman." Brown himself ultimately toured England and the United States with a panorama, or multi-scene mural, illustrating the history of slavery and freedom. One panel of his picture-history was, of course, the "resurrection" of Henry ("Box") Brown.**

Although the name of Henry Box Brown has been echoed over the land for a number of years, and the simple facts connected with his marvelous escape from slavery in a box published widely through the medium of anti-slavery papers, nevertheless it is not unreasonable to suppose that very little is generally known in relation to this case.

Briefly, the facts are these, which doubtless have never before been fully published—

Brown was a man of invention as well as a hero. In point of interest, however, his case is no more remarkable than many others. Indeed, neither before nor after escaping did he suffer one-half what many others have experienced.

He was decidedly an unhappy piece of property in the city of Richmond, Va. In the condition of a slave he felt that it would be impossible for him to remain. Full well did he know, however, that it was no holiday task to escape the vigilance of Virginia slave-hunters, or the wrath of an enraged master for committing the unpardonable sin of attempting to escape to a land of liberty. So Brown counted well the cost before venturing upon this hazardous undertaking. Ordinary modes of travel he concluded might prove

*Hunting runaway slaves with hounds was a practice that made running away a difficult and dangerous proposition. Though allowing the dogs to attack and maim slaves was illegal in some states, these sanctions were rarely enforced and vicious dogs were frequently put on the trail of runaways.*

disastrous to his hopes; he, therefore, hit upon a new invention altogether, which was to have himself boxed up and forwarded to Philadelphia direct by express. The size of the box and how it was to be made to fit him most comfortably, was of his own ordering. Two feet eight inches deep, two feet wide, and three feet long were the exact dimensions of the box, lined with baize. His resources with regard to food and water consisted of the following: One bladder of water and a few small biscuits. His mechanical implement to meet the death-struggle for fresh air, all told, was one large gimlet. Satisfied that it would be far better to peril his life for freedom in this way than to remain under the galling yoke of Slavery, he entered his box, which was safely nailed up and hooped with five hickory hoops, and was then addressed by his next friend, James A. Smith, a shoe dealer, to Wm. H. Johnson, Arch street, Philadelphia, marked, "This side up with care." In this condition he was sent to Adams' Express office in a dray, and thence by overland express to Philadelphia. It was twenty-six hours from the time he left Richmond until his arrival in the City of Brotherly Love. The notice, "This side up, &c.," did not avail with the different expressmen, who hesitated not to handle the box in the usual rough manner common to this class of men. For a while they actually had the box upside down, and had him on his head for miles. . . .

Next morning, according to arrangement, the box was at the Anti-Slavery office in due time. The witnesses present to behold the resurrection were J. M. McKim, Professor C. D. Cleveland, Lewis Thompson, and the writer. . . . All was quiet.

The door had been safely locked. The proceedings commenced. Mr. McKim rapped quietly on the lid of the box and called out, "All right!" Instantly came the answer from within, "All right, sir!"

The witnesses will never forget that moment. Saw and hatchet quickly had the five hickory hoops cut and the lid off, and the marvellous resurrection of Brown ensued. Rising up in his box, he reached out his hand saying, "How do you do, gentlemen?" The little assemblage hardly knew what to think or do at the moment. He was about as wet as if he had come up out of the Delaware. Very soon he remarked that, before leaving Richmond he had selected for his arrival-hymn (if he lived) the Psalm beginning with these words: *"I waited patiently for the Lord, and He heard my prayer."* And most touchingly did he sing the psalm, much to his own relief, as well as to the delight of his small audience.

He was then christened Henry Box Brown, and soon afterward was sent to the hospitable residence of James Mott and E. M. Davis, on Ninth street, where, it is needless to say, he met a most cordial reception from Mrs. Lucretia Mott and her household. Clothing and creature comforts were furnished in abundance, and delight and joy filled all hearts in that stronghold of philanthropy.

As he had been so long doubled up in the box he needed to promenade considerably in the fresh air, so James Mott put one of his broad-brim hats on his head and tendered him the hospitalities of his yard as well as his house, and while Brown promenaded the yard flushed with victory, great was the joy of his friends.

After his visit at Mr. Mott's, he spent two days with the writer, and then took his departure for Boston, evidently feeling quite conscious of the wonderful feat he had performed, and at the same time it may be safely said that those who witnessed this strange resurrection were not only elated at his success, but were made to sympathize more deeply than ever before with the slave. Also the noble-hearted Smith who boxed him up was made to rejoice over Brown's victory, and was thereby encouraged to render similar service to two other young bondmen, who appealed to him for deliverance. But, unfortunately, in his attempt the undertaking proved a failure. Two boxes containing the young men alluded to above, after having been duly expressed and some distance on the road, were, through the agency of the telegraph, betrayed, and the heroic young fugitives were captured in their boxes and dragged back to hopeless bondage. Consequently, through this deplorable failure, Samuel A. Smith was arrested, imprisoned, and was called upon to suffer severely.

SIC SEMPER TYRANNIS.

122ᵀᴴ REGᵗ U.S. COLORED TROOPS.

*Chapter Six*

# The Second American Revolution and the End of Slavery

The banner of the 22nd U.S. Colored Infantry shows African Americans as important fighters in the Civil War. "Sic semper tyrannis," a Latin phrase meaning "Thus always to tyrants," was used by some Southerners (including John Wilkes Booth, the murderer of Abraham Lincoln) to refer to the Union's attempt to coerce the South. But this flag depicts Southern Confederate slaveholders as the real tyrants.

The Civil War is perhaps the central event in both American and African-American history. It would never have occurred had it not been for the resistance of slaves and the many years of activism by black and white opponents of slavery in the North. For several decades, through a series of carefully orchestrated legal compromises involving slavery and its future in new western states, national statesmen kept armed conflict at bay. But with the Mexican War and the admission of territories such as Texas in the late 1840s, the slavery question could no longer be considered a sectional matter or an issue only for blacks and their sympathizers.

More and more Americans came to believe that there were two societies coexisting within their country, one slaveholding and one "free." Abolitionists influenced even those who did not care about the fate of African Americans to begin to choose sides. Controversies over fugitive slaves raised the fundamental question of civil rights: Were white Americans in the North obliged to aid slave catchers? Was it a free country if citizens—free blacks in the North—could be kidnapped on the streets and sold back to the South? Such questions helped to polarize American politics, leading to the breakdown of the old Whig and Democratic parties and the rise of the Republicans—the party of "free soil" in the West, of Abraham Lincoln, and eventually, the Union.

Radical abolitionists such as John Brown, who led an ill-fated attack on the Harpers Ferry federal arms depot in Virginia, in the hope of beginning a slave rebellion there, further polarized the debate by provoking sympathy from some northerners and condemnation by white southerners. The election of Lincoln spurred several states to call secession conventions, but many areas of the South, especially those with fewer slaves, responded less enthusiastically to the call for a new, southern confederacy. The strong, traditionally slaveholding coastal regions led the movement, and their leaders wrote an explicit endorsement of slavery into the Confederate constitution. Although the southerners justified the war in terms of their rights (and the general rights of states to run their own affairs without interference from the federal government), it was clear that slaveholding was first among those southern ways and those states' rights.

Lincoln and his party, too, justified the war on grounds other than slavery, even as he admitted that it was the sticking point between the sections. Initially, Lincoln engaged in war to oppose an illegal breakup of the United States, on behalf of those southern citizens who had not consented to leave the Union—not because of the slaves. The story of the Civil War, however, is more than that of a war for national unity or southern independence. Slavery became the focus because African Americans, in the North and South, were not contented to stay on the sidelines. They made the Civil War the culmination of their long struggle against slavery.

# Justified Rebellion

The Fugitive Slave Law, part of the Compromise of 1850 that allowed Missouri into the Union as a slave state, toughened the federal laws that not only allowed but required federal marshals to assist slave catchers in apprehending runaways. Although the number of slaves actually recaptured and sent south was not very large, examples of former slaves resisting arrest—and being aided by northern whites and blacks— made national news. One of the most spectacular cases was the "riot" in Christiana, Pennsylvania. Several slaves who had fled their master, Edward Gorsuch, enlisted the aid of a fugitive named William Parker, who was already famous for his own earlier escape, and mounted a pitched battle against Gorsuch and the authorities in which the planter was killed.

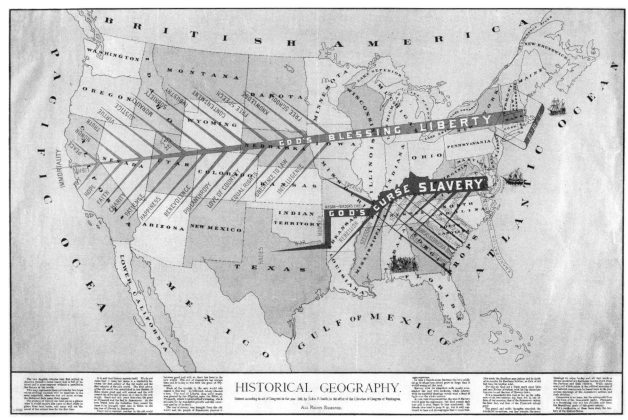

HISTORICAL GEOGRAPHY.

*This map, entitled "Historical Geography," graphically emphasizes the argument that the North and South were essentially separate countries with completely different histories—the history of the free North sprouting from Plymouth in 1620 and the slaveholding South from Jamestown in 1619. While this view of history glosses over the North's slave-owning past, the regions came to see their cultures as unique and incompatible.*

**Parker fled to Canada, where he later wrote this account of the confrontation at his house in Christiana. His language and assumptions reveal that for people like Parker, the Fugitive Slave Law, as well as slavery itself, was already a declaration of war—a war in which violence was not only justified but necessary to secure freedom. In fighting bravely, former male slaves would prove their manhood. For Parker and other abolitionists, this war was also a sacred one, justified by God. Thus it was important to accurately quote Scripture and to claim Christianity away from the masters, as Parker insists he did at the moment of highest drama. Leadership in the church proved a testing ground for leadership in the war against slaveholders.**

The leader [of the slave-catching party], Kline, replied, "I am the United States Marshal."

I then told him to take another step and I would break his neck. He again said, "I am the United States Marshal."

I told him I did not care for him nor the United States. At that he turned and went downstairs.

Pinckney said, as he turned to go down,—"Where is the use in fighting? They will take us."

Kline heard him, and said, "Yes, give up, for we can and will take you anyhow."

I told them all not to be afraid, nor to give up to any slave-holder, but to fight until death.

"Yes," said Kline, "I have heard many a negro talk as big as you and then have taken him; and I'll take you."

"You have not taken me yet," I replied; "and if you undertake it you will have your name recorded in history for this day's work."

Mr. Gorsuch then spoke, and said,—"Come, Mr. Kline, let's go up stairs and take them. We *can* take them. Come follow me, I'll go up and get my property. What's in the way? The law is in my favor, and the people are in my favor."

At that he began to ascend the stair; but I said to him,—"See here, old man, you can come up, but you can't go down again. Once up here, you are mine."

Kline then said—"Stop, Mr. Gorsuch. I will read the warrant, and then, I think, they will give up."

He then read the warrant, and said,—"Now, you see, we are commanded to take you, dead or alive; so you may as well give up at once."

"Go up, Mr. Kline," then said Mr. Gorsuch, "you are the Marshal."

Kline started, and when a little way up said, "I am coming."

I said, "Well, come on."

But he was too cowardly to show his face. He went down again and said,—"You had better give up without any more fuss, for we are bound to take you anyhow. I told you before that I was the United States Marshal, yet you will not give up. I'll not trouble the slaves. I will take you and make you pay for all."

"Well," I answered, "take me and make me pay for all. I'll pay for all."

Mr. Gorsuch then said, "You have my property."

To which I replied,—"Go in the room down there, and see if there is anything there belonging to you. There are beds and a bureau, chairs, and other things. Then go out to the barn; there you will find a cow and some hogs. See if any of them are yours."

He said, —"They are not mine; I want my men. They are here, and I am bound to have them."

This we parleyed for a time, all because of the pusillanimity of the Marshal, when he, at last, said,—"I am tired waiting on you; I see you are not going to give up. Go to the barn and fetch some straw," said he to one of his men. "I will set the house on fire, and burn them up."

"Burn us up and welcome," said I. "None but a coward would say the like. You can burn us, but you can't take us; before I give up, you will see my ashes scattered on the earth."

By this time day had begun to dawn; and then my wife came to me and asked if she should blow the horn, to bring friends to our assistance. I assented, and she went to the garret for the purpose. When the horn sounded from the garret window, one of the ruffians asked the others what it meant; and Kline said to me, "What do you mean by blowing that horn?"

The Christiana riot took place in and around this stone house owned by William Parker.

I did not answer. It was a custom with us, when a horn was blown at an unusual hour, to proceed to the spot promptly to see what was the matter. Kline ordered his men to shoot any one they saw blowing the horn. There was a peach-tree at that end of the house. Up it two of the men climbed; and when my wife went a second time to the window, they fired as soon as they heard the blast, but missed their aim. My wife then went down on her knees, and, drawing her head and body below the range of the window, the horn resting on the sill, blew blast after blast, while the shots poured thick and fast around her. They must have fired ten or twelve times. The house was of stone, and the windows were deep, which alone preserved her life.

They were evidently disconcerted by the blowing of the horn. Gorsuch said again, "I want my property, and I will have it."

"Old man," said I, "you look as if you belonged to some persuasion."

"Never mind," he answered, "what persuasion I belong to; I want my property."

While I was leaning out of the window, Kline fired a pistol at me, but the shot went too high; the ball broke the glass just above my head. I was talking to Gorsuch at the time. I seized a gun and aimed it at Gorsuch's breast, for he evidently had instigated Kline to fire; but Pinckney caught my arm and said, "Don't shoot." The gun went off, just grazing Gorsuch's shoulder. Another conversation then ensued between Gorsuch, Kline, and myself, when another one of the party fired at me but missed. Dickinson Gorsuch, I then saw, was preparing to shoot; and I told him if he

## The Right to Flee

*Anthony Burns became known around the country when a Boston abolitionist crowd tried to rescue him from jail after he was seized under the Fugitive Slave Law. During the controversy, his church in Union, Virginia, excommunicated him, and Burns replied with an eloquent defense of his actions.*

I disobeyed no law of God as revealed in the Bible. I read in Paul (1 Cor. 7:21), "But, if thou mayest be made free, use it rather." I read in Moses (Deut. 23:15, 16), "Thou shall not deliver unto his master the servant which is escaped from his master unto thee. He shall dwell with thee, even among you in that place which he shall choose in one of thy gates, where it liketh him best; thou shall not oppress him." This implies my right to flee if I feel oppressed, and debars any man from delivering me again to my professed master.

I said I was stolen. God's word declares, "He that stealeth a man and selleth him, or if he be found in his hand, he shall surely be put to death." (Ex. 21:16.) Why did you not execute God's law on the man who stole me from my mother's arms?

missed, I would show him where shooting first came from.

I asked them to consider what they would have done, had they been in our position. "I know you want to kill us," I said, for you have shot at us time and again. We have only fired twice, although we have guns and ammunition, and could kill you all if we would, but we do not want to shed blood."

"If you do not shoot any more," then said Kline, "I will stop my men from firing."

They then ceased for a time. This was about sunrise.

Mr. Gorsuch now said,—"Give up and let me have my property. Hear what the Marshal says; the Marshal is your friend. He advises you to give up without more fuss, for my property I will have."

I denied that I had his property when he replied, "You have my men."

"Am I your man?" I asked.

"No."

I then called Pinckney forward.

"Is that your man?"

"No."

Abraham Johnson I called next, but Gorsuch said he was not his man.

The only plan left was to call both Pinckney and Johnson again; for had I called the others, he would have recognized them, for they were his slaves.

Abraham Johnson said, "Does such a shrivelled up old slaveholder as you own such a nice, genteel young man as I am?"

At this Gorsuch took offence, and charged me with dictating his language. I then told him there were but five of us, which he denied, and still insisted that I had his property. One of the party then attacked the Abolitionists, affirming that, although they declared there could not be property in man, the Bible was conclusive authority in favor of property in human flesh.

"Yes," said Gorsuch, "does not the Bible say, 'Servants, obey your masters'?"

I said that it did, but the same Bible said, "Give unto your servants that which is just and equal."

At this stage of the proceedings, we went into a mutual Scripture inquiry, and bandied views in the manner of garrulous old wives.

When I spoke of duty to servants, Gorsuch said, "Do you know that?"

"Where," I asked, "do you see it in Scripture that a man should traffic in his brother's blood?"

"Do you call a nigger my brother?" said Gorsuch.

"Yes," said I.

"William," said Samuel Thompson, "he has been a class-leader."

When Gorsuch heard that, he hung his head, but said nothing. We then all joined in singing,—

"Leader, what do you say
About the judgment day?
I will die on the field of battle,
Die on the field on battle,
With glory in my soul."

Then we all began to shout, singing meantime, and shouted for a long while. Gorsuch, who was standing head bowed, said "What are you doing now?"

Samuel Thompson replied, "Preaching a sinner's funeral sermon."

"You had better give up, and come down."

I then said to Gorsuch,—"'If a brother see a sword coming, and he warn not his brother, then the brother's blood is required at his hands; but if the brother see the sword coming, and warn his brother, and his brother flee not, then his brother's blood is required at his own hand.' I see the sword coming, and, old man, I warn you to flee; if you flee not, your blood be upon your own hand."

It was now about seven o'clock.

"You had better give up," said old Mr. Gorsuch, after another while, "and come down, for I have come a long way this morning, and want my breakfast; for my property I will have, or I'll breakfast in hell. I will go up and get it."

He then started up stairs, and came far enough to see us all plainly. We were just about to fire upon him, when Dickinson Gorsuch, who was standing on the old oven, before the door, and could see into the up-stairs room through the window, jumped down and caught his father, saying,—"O father, do come down! do come down! do come down! They have guns, swords, and all kinds of weapons! They'll kill you! Do come down!"

The old man turned and left. When down with him, young Gorsuch could scarce draw breath, and the father looked more like a dead than a living man, so frightened were they at their supposed danger. The old man stood some time without saying anything; at last he said, as if soliloquizing, "I want my property, and I will have it."

Kline broke forth, "If you don't give up by fair means, you will

*We are slaves in the midst of freedom, waiting patiently, and unconcernedly—indifferently, and stupidly, for masters to come and lay claim to us, trusting to their generosity, whether or not they will own us and carry us into endless bondage.*

*—Martin Robison Delany,*
*The Condition, Elevation, Emigration,*
*and Destiny of the Colored People*
*of the United States (1852)*

have to by foul."

I told him we would not surrender on any conditions.

Young Gorsuch then said,—"Don't ask them to give up—*make* them do it. We have money, and can call men to take them. What is it that money won't buy!"

Then said Kline,—"I am getting tired waiting on you; I see you are not going to give up."

He then wrote a note and handed it to Joshua Gorsuch, saying at the same time,—"Take it, and bring a hundred men from Lancaster."

As he started, I said,—"See here! When you go to Lancaster, don't bring a hundred men,—bring five hundred. It will take all the men in Lancaster to change our purpose or take us alive."

He stopped to confer with Kline, when Pinckney said, "We had better give up."

"You are getting afraid," said I.

"Yes," said Kline, "give up like men. The rest would give up if it were not for you."

"I am not afraid," said Pinckney; "but where is the sense in fighting against so many men, and only five of us?"

The whites, at this time, were coming from all quarters, and Kline was enrolling them as fast as they came. Their numbers alarmed Pinckney, and I told him to go and sit down; but he said, "No, I will go down stairs."

I told him, if he attempted it, I should be compelled to blow out his brains. "Don't believe that any living man can take you," I said. "Don't give up to any slaveholder."

To Abraham Johnson, who was near me, I then turned. He declared he was not afraid. "I will fight till I die," he said.

At this time, Hannah, Pinckney's wife, had become impatient of our persistent course; and my wife, who brought me her message urging us to surrender, seized a corn-cutter, and declared she would cut off the head of the first one who should attempt to give up.

Another one of Gorsuch's slaves was coming along the highroad at this time, and I beckoned to him to go around. Pinckney saw him, and soon became more inspired. Elijah Lewis, a Quaker, also came along about this time: I beckoned to him, likewise; but he came straight on, and was met by Kline, who ordered him to assist him. Lewis asked for his authority, and Kline handed him the warrant. While Lewis was reading, Castner Hanway came up, and Lewis handed the warrant to him. Lewis asked Kline what Parker said.

Kline replied, "He won't give up."

Then Lewis and Hanway both said to the Marshal,—"If Parker says they will not give up, you had better let them alone, for he will kill some of you. We are not going to risk our lives"—and they turned to go away.

While they were talking, I came down and stood in the doorway, my men following behind.

Old Mr. Gorsuch said, when I appeared, "They'll come out and get away!" and he came back to the gate.

I then said to him,—"You said you could and would take us. Now you have the chance."

They were a cowardly-looking set of men.

Mr. Gorsuch said, "You can't come out here."

"Why?" said I. "This is my place. I pay rent for it. I'll let you see if I can't come out."

"I don't care if you do pay rent for it," said he. "If you come out, I will give you the contents of these"—presenting, at the same time, two revolvers, one in each hand.

I said, "Old man, if you don't go away, I will break your neck."

I then walked up to where he stood arms resting on the gate, trembling as if afflicted with palsy, and laid my hand on his shoulder, saying, "I have seen pistols before to-day." Kline now came running up, and entreated Gorsuch to come away.

"No," said the latter, "I will have my property, or go to hell."

"What do you intend to do?" said Kline to me.

"I intend to fight," said I. "I intend to try your strength."

"If you will withdraw your men," he replied, "I will withdraw mine."

I told him it was too late. "You would not withdraw when you had the chance,—you shall not now."

Kline then went back to Hanway and Lewis. Gorsuch made a signal to his men, and they all fell into line. I followed his example as well as I could; but as we were not more than ten paces apart, it was difficult to do so. At this time we numbered but ten, while there were between thirty and forty of the white men.

While I was talking to Gorsuch, his son said, "Father, will you take all this from a nigger?"

I answered him by saying that I respected old age; but that, if he would repeat that, I should knock his teeth down his throat. At this he fired upon me, and I ran up to him and knocked the pistol out of his hand, when he let the other one fall and ran in the field.

My brother-in-law, who was standing near, then said, "I can

*These slaves are escaping from Maryland's Eastern Shore and heading north to freedom. Harriet Tubman, the Underground Railroad leader, escaped from the Eastern Shore, led hundreds of Maryland slaves to freedom, and by her example inspired others to escape. When the Fugitive Slave Law was enacted in the 1850s, Tubman led her fugitives all the way to Canada.*

stop him"—and with his double-barrel gun he fired.

Young Gorsuch fell, but rose and ran on again. Pinckney fired a second time and again Gorsuch fell, but was soon up again, and running into the cornfield, lay down in the fence corner.

I returned to my men, and found Samuel Thompson talking to old Mr. Gorsuch, his master. They were both angry.

"Old man, you had better go home to Maryland," said Samuel.

"You had better give up, and come home with me," said the old man.

Thompson took Pinckney's gun from him, struck Gorsuch, and brought him to his knees. Gorsuch rose and signalled to his men. Thompson then knocked him down again, and he again rose. At this time all the white men opened fire, and we rushed upon them; when they turned, threw down their guns and ran away. We, being closely engaged, clubbed our rifles. We were too closely pressed to fire, but we found a good deal could be done with empty guns.

Old Mr. Gorsuch was the bravest of his party; he held on to his pistols until the last, while all the others threw away their weapons. I saw as many as three at a time fighting with him. Sometimes he was on his knees, then on his back, and again his feet would be where his head should be. He was a fine soldier and a brave man. Whenever he saw the least opportunity, he would take aim. While in close quarters with the whites, we could load and fire but two or three times. Our guns got bent and out of order. So damaged did they become, that we could shoot with but two or three of them. Samuel Thompson bent his gun on old Mr.

Gorsuch so badly, that it was of no use to us.

When the white men ran, they scattered. I ran after Nathan Nelson, but could not catch him. I never saw a man run faster. Returning, I saw Joshua Gorsuch coming, and Pinckney behind him. I reminded him that he would like "to take hold of a nigger." told him that now was his "chance," and struck him a blow on the side of the head, which stopped him. Pinckney came up behind, and gave him a blow which brought him to the ground; as the others passed, they gave him a kick or jumped upon him, until blood oozed out at his ears.

Nicholas Hutchings and Nathan Nelson of Baltimore County, Maryland, could outrun any men I ever saw. They and Kline were not brave, like the Gorsuches. Could our men have got them, they would have been satisfied.

One of our men ran after Dr. Pierce, as he richly deserved attention; but Pierce caught up with Castner Hanway, who rode between the fugitive and the Doctor, to shield him and some others. Hanway was told to get out of the way, or he would forfeit his life; he went aside quickly, and the man fired at the Marylander, but missed him,—he was too far off. I do not know whether he was wounded or not; but I do know that, if it had not been for Hanway, he would have been killed.

Having driven the slavocrats off in every direction, our party now turned towards their several homes. Some of us, however, went back to my house, where we found several of the neighbors.

The scene at the house beggars description. Old Mr. Gorsuch was lying in the yard in a pool of blood, and confusion reigned both inside and outside the house.

Levi Pownall said to me, "The weather is so hot and the flies are so bad, will you give me a sheet to put over the corpse?"

In reply, I gave him permission to get anything he needed from the house.

"Dickinson Gorsuch is lying in the fence-corner, and I believe he is dying. Give me something for him to drink," said Pownall, who seemed to be acting the part of the Good Samaritan.

When he returned from ministering to Dickinson, he told me he could not live.

The riot, so called, was now entirely ended. The elder Gorsuch was dead; his son and nephew were both wounded. One received a ball in his hand, near his wrist; but it only entered the skin, and he pushed it out with his thumb. Another received a ball in the fleshy part of his thigh, which had to be extracted; but neither of them were sick or crippled by the wounds. When young

*John A. Copeland was a student at Oberlin College before joining John Brown in his raid at Harpers Ferry. Of the 18 men who participated in the raid, 6 were African American.*

Gorsuch fired at me in the early part of the battle, both balls passed through my hat, cutting off my hair close to the skin, but they drew no blood. The marks were not more than an inch apart.

A story was afterwards circulated that Mr. Gorsuch shot his own slave, and in retaliation his slave shot him, but it was without foundation. His slave struck him the first and second blows; then three or four sprang upon him, and, when he became helpless, left him to pursue others. The *women put an end to him*. His slaves, so far from meeting death at his hands, are all still living.

**John A. Copeland was one of the 18 men who seized the Harpers Ferry armory in Virginia on October 16, 1859, in an attempt to secure weapons, liberate slaves, and mount an armed insurrection. While leader John Brown saw himself as a revolutionary prophet, a Moses-like figure exercising God's will, Copeland found his justification for rebellion in American history, as he reveals in this letter to his brother.**

**Copeland was hanged six days after he wrote this letter. In a deliberate insult, his body was given by the state of Virginia to a medical college for dissection—the usual fate of criminals at this time. Although there was no body to bury, 3,000 people attended a funeral for Copeland in Oberlin, Ohio, his hometown.**

Charleston, VA Dec. 10 1859
My Dear Brother:

I now take my pen to write you a few lines to let you know how I am, and in answer to your kind letter of the 5th instant. Dear Brother, I am, it is true, so situated at present as to scarcely know how to commence writing; not that my mind is filled with fear or that it has become shattered in view of my near approach to death. Not that I am terrified by the gallows which I see staring me in the face, and upon which I am soon to stand and suffer death for doing what George Washington, the so-called father of this great but slave-cursed country, was made a hero for doing while he lived, and when dead his name was immortalized, and his great and noble deed in behalf of freedom taught by parents to their children. And now, brother, for having lent my aid to a General no less brave, and engaged in a cause no less honorable and glorious, I am to suffer death. Washington entered the field to fight for the freedom of the American people—not for the white man alone, but for both black and white. Nor were they white men alone who fought for the freedom of this country. The blood of black men flowed as freely as that of white men. Yes, the very first blood that was spilt was that of a negro. It was the blood of that heroic man, (though black he was), Cyrus Attuck [Crispus Attucks]. And some of the very last blood shed was that of black men. To the truth of this, history, though prejudiced, is compelled to attest. It is true that black men did an equal share of the fighting for American Independence, and they were assured by the whites that they should share equal benefits for so doing. But after having performed their part honorably, they were by the whites most treacherously deceived—they refusing to fulfill their part of the contract. But this you know as well as I do, and I will therefore say no more in reference to the claims which we, as colored men, have on the American people.

**John Copeland may have learned his history from the first work of American history published by an African American: William Cooper Nell's *Colored Patriots of the American Revolution* (1855). At the conclusion of this work, Nell calls for a second American revolution to complete the first, describing the antislavery movement as the vanguard of a fight for the equality of all.**

The Revolution of 1776, and the subsequent struggles in our nation's history, aided, in honorable proportion, by colored Americans, have (sad, but true, confession) yet left the necessity for a second revolution, no less sublime than that of regenerating public sentiment in favor of Universal Brotherhood. To this glorious consummation, all, of every complexion, sect, sex and condition, can add their mite, and so nourish the tree of liberty, that all may be enabled to pluck fruit from its bending branches; and, in that degree to which colored Americans may labor to hasten the day, they will prove valid their claim to the title, "Patriots of the Second Revolution."

The Anti-Slavery war waged for the last twenty-five years has indeed been prolific in noble words and deeds, and is remarkable for the succession of victories, always the reward of the faithful and persevering. To compare the present with the past—those dark hours when the bugle blast was first sounded among the hills and valleys of New England,—we can hardly believe the evidence daily presented of the onward progress of those mighty principles then proclaimed to the American nation. The treatment of the colored man in this country is a

## Crimes of a Guilty Land

*John Brown impressed Americans north and south with his eloquent denunciations of slavery during his imprisonment and trial. While accurately condemning him as a fanatic, even some southerners, such as the pro-slavery Governor Henry Wise of Virginia, professed their admiration for his consistent espousal of his revolutionary beliefs. Wise himself saved his condemnation for northern men and women who sympathized with Brown, but criticized his methods. Though many of the southerners who admired Brown were slaveholders like Wise, such accusations of hypocrisy proved that sectional relations had come to a grave impasse. Thus rebels against slavery like Brown and his followers forced the issue and paved the way for the war between the states.*

*Brown himself, on his way to the gallows, criticized his own methods—but predicted that since he had failed, only a violent apocalypse would rid America of slavery:*

I John Brown am now quite *certain* that the crimes of this *guilty, land:* will never be purged *away,* but with Blood. I had *as I now think:* vainly flattered myself that without *very much* bloodshed it might be done.

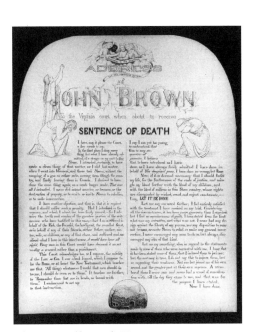

*John Brown's address to the Virginia court was widely published and he became a celebrated martyr for the antislavery cause. The writer and abolitionist Henry David Thoreau called him "an angel of light." Massachusetts governor John A. Andrew said that Brown's tactics were wrong, but "John Brown himself is right."*

*I always thought a lot of Lincoln, 'cause he had a heap of faith in de nigger ter think dat he could live on nothin at all.*

—Jacob Thomas,
a former slave interviewed
by the Works Progress
Administration in the 1930s

*Susie King Taylor was born a slave in Georgia in 1848 and was taught to read by a free black woman who ran a secret school in Savannah.*

legitimate illustration of "hating those whom we have injured," and brings to my recollection that chapter in Waverly where Fergus MacIvar replies to his friend, when being led to execution—"You see the compliment they pay to our Highland strength and courage. Here we have lain until our limbs are cramped into palsy, and now they send six soldiers with loaded muskets to prevent our taking the castle by storm." The analogy is found in the omnipotent and omnipresent influence of American pro-slavery in crushing every noble and praiseworthy aspiration of the persecuted colored man. As in nature, the smiles of summer are made sweeter by the frowns of winter, the calm of ocean is made more placid by the tempest that has preceded it, so in this moral battle, these incidental skirmishes will contribute to render the hour of victory indeed a blissful realization.

## A Welcome War

**Susie King Taylor was born a slave in Savannah, Georgia, in 1848. As a teenager, she worked as a nurse among the wounded black soldiers in South Carolina. In her *Reminiscences of My Life in Camp* (1902), she recalled how white southerners had sought to separate "Yankees," or northerners, from slaves because they feared a revolt instigated by the North.**

About this time [the autumn of 1860] I had been reading so much about the "Yankees" I was very anxious to see them. The white would tell their colored people not to go to the Yankees, for they would harness them to carts and make them pull the carts around, in the place of horses. I asked grandmother, one day, if this was true. She replied, "Certainly not!" that the white people did not want slaves to go over to the Yankees, and told then these things to frighten them. "Don't you see those signs pasted about the streets? one reading 'I am a rattlesnake, if you touch me I will strike!' Another reads, 'I am a wildcat! Beware,' etc. These are warnings to the North; so don't mind what the white people say." I wanted to see these wonderful "Yankees" so much, as I heard my parents say the Yankee was going to set all the slaves free. Oh, how those people prayed for freedom! I remember, one night, my grandmother went on into the suburbs of the city to a church meeting, and they were fervently singing this old hymn,—

"Yes, we all shall be free,
Yes, we all shall be free,

When the Lord shall appear,"—

when the police came in and arrested all who were there, saying they were planning freedom, and sang "the Lord," in place of "Yankee," to blind any one who might be listening.

**Northern African Americans saw the Civil War as a means to end slavery and to change their own unequal status in the free states. Soon after the war began, they asked to be able to enlist in the Union army. In most cases, their request was denied because the Lincoln administration sought to unify northern whites around the idea of a war for union—rather than the much less popular idea of a war against slavery, or for black rights. Blacks in Boston held a mass meeting and published their resolutions in William Lloyd Garrison's abolitionist newspaper, the *Liberator*, on May 31, 1861.**

*Resolutions of Negroe Mass Meeting*

Whereas, The traitors of the South have assailed the United States Government, with the intention of overthrowing it for the purpose of perpetrating slavery; and,

Whereas, in such a contest between the North and South—believing, as we do, that it is a contest between liberty and despotism—it is as important for each class of citizens to declare, as it is for the rulers of the Government to know, their sentiments and position; therefore,

Resolved, That our feelings urge us to say to our countrymen that we are ready to stand by and defend the Government as the equals of its white defenders—to do so with "our lives, our fortunes, and our sacred honor," for the sake of freedom and as good citizens; and we ask you to modify your laws, that we may enlist—that full scope may be given to the patriotic feelings burning in the colored man's breast—and we pledge ourselves to raise an army in the country of fifty thousand colored men.

Resolved, That more than half of the army which we could raise, being natives of the South, knowing its geography, and being acquainted with the character of the enemy, would be of incalculable service to the Government.

Resolved, That the colored women would go as nurses, seamstresses, and warriors, if need be, to crush rebellion and uphold the Government.

Resolved, That the colored people, almost without an exception, "Have their souls in arms, and all eager for the fray," and are ready to go at a moment's warning, if they are allowed to go as

SAMBO AGONISTES.
"DEY DON'T BUDGE"

*In this British cartoon from 1866 a caricatured slave is trying to budge the columns holding up the Constitution. The cartoon mocks the idea of slaves as heroes of the Civil War and the notion of former slaves seeking to change the Constitution itself through amendments that would grant them not only freedom, but civil rights.*

## Vote Republican

*Free blacks had long debated whether abolition could be achieved through the political system. William Watkins, a veteran of the antislavery struggle who had helped convince the abolitionist editor William Lloyd Garrison to oppose colonization 30 years before, wrote an articoe for the* Weekly Anglo-African *in 1859, urging blacks to vote Republican.*

Now, the Republican party is the only political party in the land in a position, numerically speaking, to strike a death-blow to American slavery—such a blow as will send it staggering to hell. It is important, then, that it assumes a defensible and right position in the present conflict. It does not deserve success, it ought not expect success, while in the occupancy of any other position. I believe it will take such a position. It *must* do so in order to preserve its distinctiveness, its vitality. If it is not right, let Abolitionists strive to make it right. More can be accomplished on the part of those who are right, by going into the party and renovating and revolutionizing it, than by standing outside harping upon a beautiful theory, but without the requisite machinery to crystalize it into practical life.

soldiers.

Resolved, That we do immediately organize ourselves into drilling companies, to the end of becoming better skilled in the use of fire-arms; so that when we shall be called upon by the country, we shall be better prepared to make ready and fitting response.

**Leaders of the antislavery movement, such as William Wells Brown, linked the effort to free the slaves with the fight for black rights in the North. In this sense, the struggle against slavery became a struggle for civil rights that continued long after the North won the war and the slaves became free. Brown was a former slave who published a narrative of his life and later traveled in England to raise money for abolition in America.**

**Brown gave this speech at the annual meeting of the American Anti-Slavery Society in May 1862. Although blacks had not at this time been allowed to enlist, Brown champions the role of "contrabands," runaway slaves in the South and border states who aided the Union army by giving them information or doing drudgery—everything from cooking to cleaning to burial detail. The situation Brown describes made it difficult for the Union to maintain that the war was, in fact, just a white man's fight. African Americans, though not yet in uniform, were already aiding the war effort. The term *contraband* was employed by military law to refer to property belonging to one side that was seized by the opponents. The military laws regarding contraband were applied to that very special kind of property—slaves who rather than being seized were running away to join the northern forces. Union officers learned firsthand that the slaves' knowledge and muscle could make a difference in the war. To Brown in 1862, schemes to colonize freed blacks in another country seemed even more hypocritical than ever.**

All I demand for the black man is, that the white people shall take their heels off his neck, and let him have a chance to rise by his own efforts. One of the first things that I heard when I arrived in the free States—and it was the strangest thing to me that I heard—was, that the slaves cannot take care of themselves. I came off without any education. Society did not take me up; I took myself up. I did not ask society to take me up. All I asked of the white people was, to get out of the way, and give me a chance to

come from the South to the North. That was all I asked, and I went to work with my own hands. And that is all I demand for my brethren of the South to-day—that they shall have an opportunity to exercise their own physical and mental abilities. Give them that, and I will leave the slaves to take care of themselves, and be satisfied with the result.

Now, Mr. President, I think that the present contest has shown clearly that the fidelity of the black people of this country to the cause of freedom is enough to put to shame every white man in the land who would think of driving us out of the country, provided freedom shall be proclaimed. I remember well, when Mr. Lincoln's proclamation went forth, calling for the first 75,000 men, that among the first to respond to that call were the colored men. A meeting was held in Boston, crowded as I never saw a meeting before; meetings were held in Rhode Island and Connecticut, in New York and Philadelphia, and throughout the West, responding to the President's call. Although the colored men in many of the free States were disfranchised, abused, taxed without representation, their children turned out of the schools, nevertheless, they went on, determined to try to discharge their duty to the country, and to save it from the tyrannical power of the slave-holders of the South. But the cry went forth—"We won't have the Negroes; we won't have anything to do with them; we won't fight with them; we won't have them in the army, nor about us." Yet scarcely had you got into conflict with the South, when you were glad to receive news that contrabands brought. The first telegram announcing any news from the disaffected district commences

## The Irrepressible Conflict

*From the beginning of the war, Frederick Douglass spoke enthusiastically for the Union—and urged that black men be permitted to fight in the army. Two of his sons, Charles and Lewis, eventually did serve. He wrote the following in an editorial in his magazine,* Douglass' Monthly, *in August 1861.*

We talk the irrepressible conflict, and practically give the lie to our talk. We wage war against slaveholding rebels, and yet protect and augment the motive which has moved the slaveholders to rebellion. We strike at the effect, and leave the cause unharmed. Fire will not burn it out of us—water cannot wash it out of us, that this war with the slave-holders can never be brought to a desirable termination until slavery, the guilty cause of all our national troubles, has been totally and forever abolished.

*These trading cards were issued by abolitionists to encourage black men to enlist in the Union army and to celebrate the courage of black soldiers. The collection of all 12 cards tells the story of a slave who is sold away from his family, whipped by his new owner, runs away, and joins the Union army; the last cards in the series portray his victorious fight for liberty.*

with—"A contraband just in from Maryland tells us" so much. The last telegram, in to-day's paper, announces that a contraband tells us so much about Jefferson Davis and Mrs. Davis and the little Davises. The nation is glad to receive the news from the contraband. We have an old law with regard to the mails, that a Negro shall not touch the mails at all; and for fifty years the black man has not had the privilege of touching the mails of the United States with his little finger; but we are glad enough now to have the Negro bring the mail in his pocket! The first thing asked of a contraband is—"Have you got a newspaper?—what's the news?" And the news is greedily taken in, from the lowest officer or soldier in the army, up to the Secretary of War. They have tried to keep the Negro out of the war, but they could not keep him out, and now they drag him in, with his news, and are glad to do so. General Wool says the contrabands have brought the most reliable news. Other Generals say their information can be relied upon. The Negro is taken as a pilot to guide the fleet of General Burnside through the inlets of the South. The black man welcomes your armies and your fleets, takes care of your sick, is ready to do anything, from cooking up to shouldering the musket; and yet these would-be patriots and professed lovers of the land talk about driving the Negro out!

**Confederates tried various ways of preventing slaves from becoming a disloyal force in their midst. They moved slaves south, away from invading Union armies; they passed a law allowing one white man to stay at home, despite the military draft, for every 20 slaves, to ensure that the slave population was supervised. The Georgia whites who wrote the following letter estimated that their county had lost 20,000 slaves to the Union forces. The usual punishments did not scare the slaves enough, so they asked, in conclusion, that runaways be considered "traitors" and executed under military law. In doing so, they were forced to admit that slaves "constitute a part of the Body politic." Slaves were not acting like slaves— they were acting like citizens, like men at war.**

*[Liberty County, Ga. August 1, 1862]*

General: The undersigned Citizens of Liberty County of the Fifteenth District, would respectfully present for your consideration a subject of grave moment, not to themselves only but to their fellow Citizens of the Confederate States, who occupy not only our territory immediately bordering on that of the old

United States, but whole line of our sea coast from Virginia to Texas. We allude to the escape of our Slaves across the border lines landward, and out to the vessels of the enemy Seaward, & to their being also enticed off by those who having made their escape, return for that purpose, and not unfrequently, attended by the enemy. The injury inflicted upon the interests of the citizens of the Confederate States by this now constant drain is immense; independent of the forcible seizure of Slaves by the enemy whenever it lies in his power; and to which we now make no allusion, as the indemnity for this loss, will in due time occupy the attention of our Government.—From ascertained losses on certain parts of our Coast, we may set down as a low estimate, the number of Slaves absconded & enticed off from our Seaboard as 20,000 & their value as from $12 to 15 million of Dollars, to which loss—may be added the insecurity of the property along our borders & the demoralization of the negroes that remain, which increases with the continuance of the evil & may finally result in perfect disorganization and rebellion.—

The absconding Negroes hold the position of Traitors, since they go over to the enemy & afford him aid & comfort, by revealing the condition of the districts and cities from which they come, & aiding him in erecting fortifications & raising provisions for his support: and now that the United States have allowed their introduction into their Army & Navy, aiding the enemy by enlisting under his banners & increasing his resources in men, for our annoyance & destruction. Negroes occupy the position of Spies also, since they are employed in secret expeditions for obtaining information, by transmission of newspapers & by other modes; and act as guides to expeditions on the land & as pilots to their vessels on the waters of our inlets and rivers.—

They have proved of great value, thus far; to the Coast operations of the enemy, & without their assistance, he could not have accomplished as much for our injury & annoyance as he has done; and unless some measures shall be adopted to prevent the escape of the negroes to the enemy, the threat of an Army of trained Africans for the coming fall & winter's campaigns may become a reality. Meanwhile the counties along the Seaboard will become exhausted of the Slave population which should be retained as far as possible for the raising of provisions & supplies for our forces on the Coast.—

*The importance of slavery to the Confederate cause is evident on the Confederate currency. The bills were decorated with pictures of slaves engaged in the agricultural activities, such as planting and harvesting cotton, that were vital to the southern economy.*

### Running to Safety

*Mary Barbour, a former slave interviewed by a WPA writer in the 1930s, remembered her family fleeing to Union lines.*

One of de fust things dat I 'members wuz my pappy wakin' me up in de middle o'de night, dressin' me in de dark, all de time tellin' me ter keep quiet. One o'de twins hollered some an' pappy put his hand ober its mouth ter keep it quiet. Atter we wuz dressed he went outside an' peeped roun' fer a minute den he comed back an' got us. We snook out o' de house an' long de woods path, pappy totin' one of de twins an' holdin' me by de han' an' mammy carryin' de odder two.

I reckons dat I will always 'member dat walk, wid de bushes slappin' my laigs, de win' sighin in de trees, an' de hoot owls an' whip-poorwills hollerin' at each other from de big trees. I wuz half asleep an' skeered stiff, but in a little while we pass de plum thicket an' dar am de mules an' wagin.

Dar am er quilt in de bottom o' de wagin, an' on dis day lays we youngins. An' pappy an' mammy gits on de board cross de front an' drives off down de road. We trabels all night an' hid in de woods all day. When er gits ter New Bern de Yankees takes de mules an wagin. My pappy wuz a shoemaker, so he makes Yankee boots, an' we gits 'long pretty good.

## "Smoked Yankees"

*White southerners learned that a revolution had truly occurred when black soldiers entered their towns. N. B. Sterrett, a black soldier, took joy in the fear shown by former masters.*

The introduction of a colored regiment here was perfectly exasperating to the citizens. I heard them calling in all manner of names that were never applied to the Deity, to deliver them from the hands of the *smoked Yankees*. But their prayers in this case were like all others offered by rebel hearts; and the next thing they saw was the *smoked Yankees* marching some of their fellow citizens to jail at the point of a bayonet.

# Emancipation

**By seceding from the Union, rebel southerners forfeited their right to have their slaves returned through the aid of federal agents. By the summer of 1862, they lost all federal protection of their slave property when President Lincoln decided to free slaves in the seceding states. He waited until an optimistic moment—after the Battle of Antietam—and was careful to present the decision as a way to win the war, rather than a change in the aims of the war. It is important to note that he did not free slaves in the slaveholding border states—areas that had not taken up arms against the Union. Moreover, in the preliminary Emancipation Proclamation below, which Lincoln issued on September 22, he did not actually free *any* slaves. It meant only that slavery would end wherever the Union army managed to gain control.**

**Ever since the Civil War, Americans have debated the importance of the Emancipation Proclamation. Eventually, Lincoln did come to see the abolition of slavery as part of what the Civil War was all about: a "new birth of freedom," as he later put it in the Gettysburg Address. In a sense, though, the proclamation made official what was already happening. The Civil War, like the American Revolution, upset slavery wherever armies clashed in the South, as tens of thousands, and eventually hundreds of thousands, of slaves left their homes—and freed themselves.**

I, Abraham Lincoln, President of the United States of America, and Commander-in-chief of the Army and Navy thereof, do hereby proclaim and declare that hereafter, as heretofore, the war will be prosecuted for the object of practically restoring the constitutional relation between the United States, and each of the states, and the people thereof, in which states that relation is, or may be suspended, or disturbed.

That it is my purpose, upon the next meeting of Congress to again recommend the adoption of a practical measure tendering pecuniary aid to the free acceptance or rejection of all slave-states, so called, the people whereof may not then be in rebellion against the United States, and which states, may then have voluntarily adopted, or thereafter may voluntarily adopt, immediate, or gradual abolishment of slavery within their respective limits; and that the effort to colonize persons of African descent, with their consent, upon this continent, or elsewhere, with the previously obtained consent of the Governments existing there, will be continued.

That on the first day of January in the year of our Lord, one thousand eight hundred and sixty-three, all persons held as slaves within any state, or designated part of a state, the people whereof shall then be in rebellion against the United States shall be then, thenceforward, and forever free; and the executive government of the United States, including the military and naval authority thereof, will recognize and maintain the freedom of such persons, and will do no act or acts to repress such persons, or any of them, in any efforts they may make for their actual freedom.

That the executive will, on the first day of January aforesaid, by proclamation, designate the States, and parts of states, if any, in which the people thereof respectively, shall then be in rebellion against the United States; and the fact that any state, or the people thereof shall, on that day be, in good faith represented in the Congress of the United States, by members chosen thereto, at elections wherein a majority of the qualified voters of such state shall have participated, shall, in the absence of strong countervailing testimony, be deemed conclusive evidence that such state and the people thereof, are not in rebellion against the United States. . . .

And the executive will in due time recommend that all citizens of the United States who shall have remained loyal thereto throughout the rebellion, shall (upon restoration of the constitutional relation between the United States, and their respective states, and people, if that relation shall have been suspended or disturbed) be compensated for all losses by the acts of the United States, including the loss of slaves.

**The effects of the Emancipation Proclamation were soon felt when the number of "contrabands" finding their way to the armies increased, as a Union general in Tennessee reported to his superior officers.**

*Lagrange, Tenn., March 27th 1863.*

Sir—I wrote a few days ago asking instructions with regard to the large number of contrabands now finding their way into our Camps—The evil is a most perplexing one. Whole families of them are stampeding and leaving their masters, and I am applied to daily for the return of those belonging to loyal Masters. I know that our General Orders do not permit me to yield to such applications: but something should be done to shield our service from the charge of furnishing an Asylum to the Servants of loyal men

## Unequal Rights

*One soldier of the 54th Massachusetts Infantry wrote home from South Carolina about the unjust terms of black service.*

I am not willing to fight for anything less than the white man fights for. If the white man cannot support his family on seven dollars per month, I cannot support mine on the same amount.

And I am not willing to fight for this Government for money alone. Give me my rights, the rights that this Government owes me, the same rights that the white man has.

*The majority of the African-American troops who fought in the Civil War, such as these teamsters photographed near Cobb Hill, Virginia, were former slaves from the South.*

**Teamster**

Wagon driver or loader

living in districts not affected by the emancipation proclamation. Very Respectfully Your obed[ien]t Servt.

Wm. Sooy Smith

**The proclamation did make it easier for Lincoln and his generals to enlist former slaves in the army. One of the first of those regiments was the First South Carolina Volunteers, raised on the Sea Islands, which had fallen into Union hands early in the war. When emancipation became official on January 1, 1863, former slaves—now soldiers—held a celebration with their officers. Charlotte Forten, a schoolteacher who traveled south to teach the freedmen, wrote of the celebration in her journal.**

Thursday, New Year's Day, 1863. The most glorious day this nation has yet seen, *I* think. . . . We stopped at Beaufort, and then proceeded to Camp Saxton, the camp of the 1st Reg.[iment] S.[outh] C.[arolina] Vol[unteer]s. . . The meeting was held in a beautiful grove, a live-oak grove, adjoining the camp. . . . As I sat on the stand and looked around on the various groups, I thought I had never seen a sight so beautiful. There were the black soldiers, in their blue coats and scarlet pants, the officers of this and other regiments in their handsome uniforms, and crowds of lookers-on, men, women and children, grouped in various attitudes, under the trees. The faces of all wore a happy, eager, expectant look. The exercises commenced by a prayer from Rev. Mr. Fowler, Chaplain of the Reg. An ode written for the occasion by Prof. Zachos, originally a Greek, now Sup.[erintendent] of Paris Island, was read by himself, and then sung by the whites. Col. H.[igginson] introduced Dr. Brisbane in a few elegant and graceful words. He (Dr. B.) read the President's Proclamation, which was warmly cheered. Then the beautiful flags presented by Dr. Cheever's Church were presented to Col. H. for the Reg. in an excellent and enthusiastic speech, by Rev. Mr. French. Immediately at the conclusion, some of the colored people—of their own accord sang "My Country Tis of Thee." It was a touching and beautiful incident, and Col. Higginson, in accepting the flags made it the occasion of some happy remarks. He said that *that* tribute was far more effecting than any speech he c'ld make. He spoke for some time, and all that he said was grand, glorious. . . A Hymn written I believe, by Mr. Judd, was sung, and then all the people united with the Reg. in singing "John Brown." . . . The Dress Parade—the first I have ever seen—delighted me. It was a brilliant sight—the lone line of men in their brilliant uniforms, with bayonets gleaming in the sunlight. The Col. looked splendid. The Dr. said the men went through the drill remarkably well. It seemed to me nothing c'ld be more perfect. To me it was a grand triumph—the black regiment doing itself honor in the sight of the white officers, many of whom, doubtless "came to scoff." It was typical of what the race, so long down-trodden and degraded will yet achieve on this continent.

**Thomas Wentworth Higginson, colonel of the First South Carolina Volunteers, led his regiment of freed slaves in a series of raids in Georgia and Florida. In this official report, Higginson described his regiment's raid on the St. Mary's River that forms the border between Georgia and Florida.**

Nobody knows anything about these men who has not seen them in battle. I find that I myself knew nothing. There is a fiery energy about them beyond anything of which I have ever read, except it be the French Zouaves. It requires the strictest discipline to hold them in hand. During our first attack on the river, before I had got them all penned below, they crowded at the open ends of the steamer, loading and firing with inconceivable rapidity, and shouting to each other, "Never give it up." When collected into the hold they actually fought each other for places at the few port-holes from which they could fire on the enemy. Meanwhile the black gunners, admirably trained by Lieutenants Stockdale and O'Neil, both being accomplished artillerists, and Mr. Heron, of the gunboat, did their duty without the slightest protection and with great coolness amid a storm of shot. . . .

No officer in this regiment now doubts that the key to the successful prosecution of this war lies in the unlimited employment of black troops. Their superiority lies simply in the fact that they know the country, while white troops do not, and, moreover, that they have peculiarities of temperament, position, and motive

## Striking Back at the South

*Women as well as men played key roles in the Union army's effort. The Boston Commonwealth reported in July 1863 how Harriet Tubman turned her expertise in guiding slaves out of the South to bringing Union forces into the South—and liberating slaves at home.*

Col. Montgomery and his gallant band of 800 black soldiers, under the guidance of a black woman, dashed into the enemies' country, struck a bold and effective blow, destroying millions of dollars worth of commissary stores, cotton and lordly dwellings, and striking terror to the heart of rebeldom, brought off near 800 slaves and thousands of dollars worth of property, without losing a man or receiving a scratch!

*The troops of the 14th U.S. Colored Infantry at Ship Island, Mississippi, stand in formation. The Emancipation Proclamation, in addition to freeing the slaves in the rebellious states, allowed black soldiers to enlist in the Union army. Black troops made up from 10 to 12 percent of the Union forces by the end of the war.*

which belong to them alone. Instead of leaving their home and families to fight they are fighting for their home and families, and they show the resolution and the sagacity which a personal purpose gives. It would have been madness to attempt, with the bravest white troops, what I have successfully accomplished with black ones.

**Colonel Higginson, in his memoir *Army Life in a Black Regiment*, described the speeches made by some of his soldiers to each other in camp in 1862. In 19th-century America, speeches were often made by men standing on tree stumps; humorous monologues—early stand-up comedy—also came to be known as stump speeches.**

The most eloquent, perhaps, was Corporal Price Lambkin, just arrived from Fernandina, who evidently had a previous reputation among them. His historical references were very interesting. He reminded them that he had predicted this war ever since Fremont's time [Fremont had been the Republican Presidential candidate in 1856], to which some of the crowd assented; he gave a very intelligent account of that Presidential campaign, and then described most impressively the secret anxiety of the slaves in Florida to know all about President Lincoln's election, and told how they all refused to work on the fourth of March [the date of Lincoln's inauguration as President in 1861], expecting their freedom to date from that day. He finally brought out one of the few really impressive appeals for the American flag that I have ever heard. "Our mas'rs dey hab lib under de flag, dey got dere wealth under it, and ebryting beautiful for dere chilen. Under it dey hab grind us up, and put us in dere pocket for money. But de fus' minute dey tink dat ole flag mean freedom for we colored people, dey pull it right down, and run up de rag ob dere own." (Immense applause.) "But we'll neber desert de ole flag, boys, neber; we hab lib under it for *eighteen hundred sixty-two years*, and we'll die for it now." With which overpowering discharge of chronology-at-long-range, this most effective of stump-speeches closed. I see already with relief that there will be small demand in this regiment for harangues from the officers; give the men an empty barrel for a stump, and they will do their own exhortation.

# Liberation

**The Union army counted 178,975 black men among its ranks. They came especially from those states and counties where**

slaves could reach Union lines. So many fled that by the end of the war a desperate Confederacy actually began to enlist slaves in the Confederate army. The loss of slaves to Union lines hurt the Confederate war effort. Sixty thousand African Americans died in Union uniforms at a time when numbers greatly mattered.

African-American soldiers also came from the North—more than 32,000 of them, more than two-thirds of the northern free black male population between the ages of 18 and 45. Because Massachusetts was the first to form a black regiment, many black northerners from other states served under the Massachusetts banner. One of these was Philadelphia's Edward D. Washington, who wrote a letter to the *Christian Recorder,* a national black newspaper published in his hometown. He had been wounded at the defeat at Fort Wagner, South Carolina, when the 54th Massachusetts, led by Colonel Robert Gould Shaw, charged a Confederate fort and proved to skeptical northerners that black soldiers would fight to the death as willingly as whites. Given such proof of bravery, Washington wondered why white soldiers received better wages as soldiers.

It is with pleasure that I now seat myself to inform you concerning our last battle: thus we were in Co. B, on the 20th of Feb. Mr. Editor, I am not sitting down to inform you about this battle without knowing something about it.

The battle took place in a grove called Olustee, with the different regiments as follows: First was the 8th U.S. [Colored Infantry]; they were cut up badly, and they were the first colored regiment in the battle. The next was the 54th Mass., which I belong to; the next were the 1st N[orth] C[arolina]. In they went and fired a few rounds, but they soon cleared out; things were too warm for them. The firing was very warm, and it continued for about three hours and a half. The 54th was the last off the field. When the 1st N. C. found out it was so warm they soon left, and then there were none left to cover the retreat. But J[ames M.] Walton, of the 54th, of our company, with shouts and cheers, cried, "Give it to them, my brave boys! Give it to them!" As I turned around, I observed Col. E[dward] N. Hallowell standing with a smile upon his countenance, as though the boys were playing a small game of ball.

There was none left but the above named, and Lieut. Col. [Henry N.] Hooper, and Col. [James] Montgomery; those were the only officers left with us. If we had been like those regiments that were ahead, I think not only in my own mind, but in the minds of the field officers, such as Col. Hooper and Col. Montgomery, that we would have suffered much less, is plain to be seen, for the enemy had taken three or four of their [artillery] pieces.

When we got there we rushed in double-quick, with a command from the General, "Right into line." We commenced with a severe firing, and the enemy soon gave way for some two hundred yards. Our forces were light, and we were compelled to fall back with much dissatisfaction.

Now it seems strange to me that we do not receive the same pay and rations as the white soldiers. Do we not fill the same ranks? Do we not cover the same space of ground? Do we not take up the same length of ground in a grave-yard that others do? The ball does not miss the black man and strike the white, nor the white and strike the black. But, sir, at that time there is no distinction made; they strike one as much as another. The black men have to go through the same hurling of musketry, and same belching of cannonading as white soldiers do.

**As the Union army penetrated deeper into southern territory, black soldiers helped liberate the slaves; they also helped former slaves set up new institutions and demand their rights as citizens under the new governments that began to form in 1865. The soldier who wrote this letter arrived in Wilmington, North Carolina, early in 1865.**

On the 21st, we built a line, and bivouacked for the night; being only four miles from the largest and oldest city in the State. We asked ourselves as well as others, "How would you like to march through Wilmington tomorrow, February 22d, the anniversary of the birthday of Washington?" The answer was, "It would be the proudest moment of my life!". . . The 22d came, and a more lovely day I never saw. By half pa[s]t six o'clock we were on the move, as General Hoke had evacuated during the night, and one hour's march brought us on the corporation line of Wilmington, when large volumes of smoke were seen rising in the eastern part of the city. For a time, we thought Hoke had set fire to the city as he went through. But not so. It was the burning of cotton and turpentine at and near the Wilmington and Weldon Railroad. The column halted for a few moments, when the mayor met General [Alfred] Terry, and begged for protection. We finally moved, and entered the blockaded city of the Confederacy—the place where

all the southern and some of the northern men have made their piles of
money—the once [rising] city of the
Confederacy; the place noted for its
slave market! But now, alas! we march
through these fine thoroughfares,
where once the slave was forbid[den]
being out after nine P. M., or to puff a
'regalia' [to wear fancy clothes] or to
walk with a cane, or to ride in a car-
riage! Negro soldiers! with banners
floating! with their splendid brass
bands and drum corps, discoursing the
National airs and marches!—the col-

Like the soldiers in this scene, black
troops helped liberate numerous communities of slaves in the deep South. From
among these black troops emerged some
of the first southern, black political
leaders during the Reconstruction era.

ored division of the 25th army corps, commanded by General
Charles J. Payne. It would be a mere attempt for one such as
myself to describe the manner in which the colored people of
Wilmington welcomed the Union troops—cheer after cheer they
gave us—they had prayed long for their deliverance, and the 22d
day of February, 1865, realized their earnest hopes. Were they not
happy that day? Free, for evermore! The streets were crowded
with them, old and young; they shook hands with the troops, and
some exclaimed, "The chain is broken!" "Joy! Freedom today!"
"Hurrah for Uncle Abe!"

"There goes my son!" said a lady. "Which one?" asked a corporal. "That one, just gone ahead!" And, sure enough, it was her son.
She overtook him and embraced him; and how proudly she felt,
none but those similarly situated can ever feel. The man knew that
his mother was living when he entered the service, for some friend
had so informed him. He had left his home a slave, but had
returned in the garb of a Union soldier, free, a man. Similar incidents have happened in other colored regiments. At one corner,
near the market, the colored people had boxes of tobacco which
they distributed to the troops as they passed. At almost every door
was a bucket of water and in many places, ladies gave bread and
meat to the boys, saying, "Tis the best we have." The farther we
advanced, the more numerous the people. At one corner, my
attention was attracted to a crowd who were "jumping for joy!"
One old man among them said he was nearly ninety-three years
old, and had not been in the street since last July; but hearing the
music of the Union troops, it had revived him, and he felt so
happy that he came out; and there he stood, with his long white
locks and his wrinkled cheeks, saying, "Welcome, welcome!"

# Timeline

**1619**
First Africans arrive in Virginia

**1660–64**
Maryland and Virginia pass laws recognizing and regulating permanent slavery

**1669**
Fundamental Constitutions of the Carolinas permits slavery

**1676**
Bacon's Rebellion in Virginia: slaves and indentured servants join to fight, causing whites to strengthen the slave system

**1712**
Slave rebellion in New York City

**1739**
Stono Rebellion in South Carolina

**1741**
Arson conspiracy in New York; 18 hanged, 70 sold into slavery

**1756–63**
Seven Years' War rages in Europe while the related conflict, the French and Indian War, which began in 1754, continues in North America

**March 5, 1770**
Crispus Attucks killed in the Boston Massacre

**1773**
Massachusetts slaves petition the legislature for freedom

Phillis Wheatley publishes her *Poems on Various Subjects, Religious and Moral*

**1775–83**
American Revolution; slaves fight on both sides

**1775**
Lord Dunmore offers freedom to slaves who will join the British forces; George Washington orders recruiters to accept free blacks in the Patriot forces

**July 4, 1776**
Declaration of Independence signed by the Continental Congress, without the passage written by Thomas Jefferson condemning the slave trade

**1780**
Pennsylvania becomes the first state to pass a gradual emancipation act

**1784**
Connecticut and Rhode Island enact gradual abolition schemes

**1787**
Richard Allen and Absalom Jones found the Free African Society in Philadelphia, the first of the black benevolent societies in the North

**1787**
Thomas Jefferson publishes his *Notes on the State of Virginia*, in English, arguing that Africans are innately inferior to whites

**1788**
U.S. Constitution ratified by the required 10 of the 13 original states

**1791**
Benjamin Banneker sends his almanac and letter to Secretary of State Thomas Jefferson

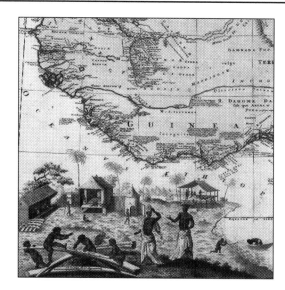

NEW-YORK, 21 April 1783.

THIS is to certify to whomsoever it may concern, that the Bearer hereof *Cato Ramsay* a Negro, reforted to the British Lines, in confequence of the Proclamations of Sir William Howe, and Sir Henry Clinton, late Commanders in Chief in America; and that the faid Negro has hereby his Excellency Sir Guy Carleton's Permiffion to go to Nova-Scotia, or wherever elfe he may think proper.

*By Order of Brigadier General Birch,*

**1793–1801**

Haitian Revolution: free mulattoes and slaves join to overthrow the French and abolish slavery on the island of Saint-Domingue

**1799**

New York enacts gradual emancipation

**1800**

Gabriel's Rebellion in Virginia

**January 1, 1808**

Slave trade made illegal by U.S. Congress

**1815**

Paul Cuffe sails to Sierra Leone with 38 African-American settlers

**July 4, 1816**

Slave revolt fails in Camden, South Carolina

**December 1816**

American Colonization Society founded in Washington, D.C.

**1822**

Denmark Vesey's plot for a slave revolt in Charleston, South Carolina, is discovered

**1827**

*Freedom's Journal*, the first African-American newspaper, published in New York by Samuel Cornish and John Russwurm

**July 4, 1827**

All slaves freed in the state of New York

**1829**

David Walker publishes his *Appeal to the Colored Citizens of the World* in Boston

**1830**

First National Negro Convention meets in Philadelphia

**January 1, 1831**

William Lloyd Garrison publishes the first issue of the *Liberator*, calling for immediate emancipation of all slaves

**August 22, 1831**

Nat Turner leads a bloody but unsuccessful slave rebellion in Southampton, Virginia

**1835**

Slavery abolished in Great Britain and its colonies

**1838**

Frederick Douglass escapes from slavery

**1839**

Slave revolt aboard the Cuban ship *La Amistad*

**1845**

*Narrative of the Life of Frederick Douglass* is published

**1849**

Harriet Tubman escapes from slavery, begins working for the Underground Railroad, helping other slaves to flee the South

**1850**

Fugitive Slave Law passed as part of the Compromise of 1850

**1851**

Slave riot in Christiana, Pennsylvania, results in the death of slaveholder Edward Gorsuch; William Parker flees to Canada

**1855**

William Cooper Nell publishes *Colored Patriots of the American Revolution*

**October 16, 1859**

John Brown leads abolitionist raid on the federal arms depot at Harpers Ferry, Virginia

**November 1860**

Abraham Lincoln is elected 16th President of the United States

**1861–65**

Civil War

**1862**

Harriet Jacobs publishes *Incidents in the Life of a Slave Girl*

**September 22, 1862**

Abraham Lincoln issues the preliminary Emancipation Proclamation

**January 1, 1863**

Emancipation Proclamation goes into effect, freeing slaves in seceding states

**1865**

The 13th Amendment to the U.S. Constitution, abolishing slavery, is passed by Congress and later ratified by the states

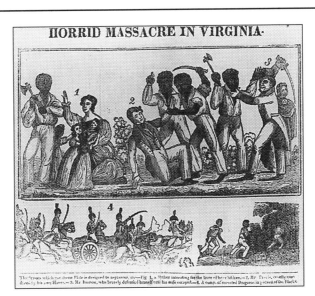

# Further Reading

Aptheker, Herbert. *American Negro Slave Revolts.* 4th ed. New York: International Publishers, 1983.

Berlin, Ira. *Many Thousands Gone: The First Two Centuries of American Slavery.* Cambridge: Harvard University Press, 1998.

Berlin, Ira, et al., eds. *Free at Last: A Documentary History of Slavery, Freedom and the Civil War.* New York: New Press, 1992.

Blassingame, John, ed. *Slave Testimony.* Baton Rouge: Louisiana State University Press, 1981.

Douglass, Frederick. *My Bondage and My Freedom.* 1855. Reprint, New York: Dover, 1969.

Frankel, Noralee. *Break Those Chains at Last: African Americans 1860–1880.* New York: Oxford University Press, 1996.

Franklin, John Hope, and Loren Schweninger. *Runaway Slaves: Rebels on the Plantation,1790–1860.* New York: Oxford University Press, 1999.

Gates, Henry Louis, Jr., ed. *The Classic Slave Narratives.* New York: Mentor, 1987.

Genovese, Eugene D. *From Rebellion to Revolution: African American Slave Revolts in the Making of the New World.* 1979. Reprint, New York: Vintage, 1981.

Harding, Vincent. *There Is a River: The Black Struggle for Freedom in America.* New York: Harcourt Brace, 1981.

Hinks, Peter P. *To Awaken My Afflicted Brethren: David Walker and the Problem of Antebellum Slave Resistance.* University Park: Pennsylvania State University Press, 1997.

Horton, James Oliver, and Lois E. Horton. *In Hope of Liberty: Culture, Community and Protest Among Northern Free Blacks, 1700–1860.* New York: Oxford University Press, 1996.

Huggins, Nathan Irvin. *Black Odyssey.* Rev. ed. New York: Vintage, 1995.

Jones, Howard. *Mutiny on the Amistad the Saga of a Slave Revolt and Its Impact on American Abolition, Law, and Diplomacy.* New York: Oxford University Press, 1987.

Kaplan, Sidney, and Emma Nogrady Kaplan. *The Black Presence in the Era of the American Revolution.* Rev. ed. Amherst: University of Massachusetts Press, 1987.

Littlefield, Daniel C. *Revolutionary Citizens: African Americans 1776–1804.* New York: Oxford University Press, 1997.

Litwack, Leon. *North of Slavery.* Chicago: University of Chicago Press, 1961.

Mayer, Henry. *All On Fire: William Lloyd Garrison and the Abolition of Slavery.* New York: St. Martin's, 1998.

McFeeley, William S. *Frederick Douglass.* New York: Norton, 1991.

McPherson, James M., ed. *The Negro's Civil War.* New York: Ballantine, 1991.

Nash, Gary B. *Race and Revolution.* Madison, Wis.: Madison House, 1990.

Osofsky, Gilbert, ed. *Puttin' On Ole Massa: The Slave Narratives of Henry Bibb, William Wells Brown, and Solomon Northup.* New York: Harper & Row, 1969.

Painter, Nell Irvin. *Sojourner Truth: A Life, A Symbol.* New York: Norton, 1996.

Pease, Jane H., and William H. Pease. *They Who Would Be Free: Blacks' Search for Freedom, 1830–1861.* Reprint, Urbana: University of Illinois Press, 1990.

Porter, Dorothy, ed. *Early Negro Writing, 1770–1837.* Boston: Beacon, 1971.

Quarles, Benjamin. *Black Abolitionists.* New York: Oxford University Press, 1969.

———. *The Negro in the American Revolution.* Chapel Hill: University of North Carolina Press, 1961.

Redkey, Edwin S., ed. *A Grand Army of Black Men: Letters from African-American Soldiers in the Union Army, 1861–1865.* New York: Cambridge University Press, 1992.

Ripley, C. Peter, ed. *Witness for Freedom: African American Voices on Race, Slavery, and Emancipation.* Chapel Hill: University of North Carolina Press, 1993.

Rose, Willie Lee. *A Documentary History of Slavery in North America.* New York: Oxford University Press, 1976.

Salvatore, Nick. *We All Got History: The Memory Books of Amos Webber.* New York: Vintage, 1997.

Smith, Billy G., and Richard Wojtowicz, eds. *Blacks Who Stole Themselves: Advertisements from the Pennsylvania Gazette, 1728–1790.* Philadelphia: University of Pennsylvania Press, 1989.

Sterling, Dorothy. *The Making of an Afro-American: Martin Robison Delany, 1812–1885.* Garden City, N.Y.: Doubleday, 1971.

Sterling, Dorothy, ed. *We Are Your Sisters: Black Women in the Nineteenth Century.* New York: Norton, 1984.

Walker, David. *David Walker's Appeal: In Four Articles, Together with a Preamble, to the Coloured Citizens of the World, but Particularly, and Very Expressly, to Those of the United States of America.* Rev. ed. New York: Hill & Wang, 1995.

White, Deborah Gray. *Let My People Go: African Americans 1804–1860.* New York: Oxford University Press, 1996.

White, Shane, and Graham White. *Stylin': African American Expressive Culture from Its Beginnings to the Zoot Suit.* Ithaca, N.Y.: Cornell University Press, 1998.

Wood, Peter H. *Strange New Land: African Americans 1617–1776.* New York: Oxford University Press, 1996.

# Text Credits

## Main Text

pp. 18–20 Olaudah Equiano, *The Interesting Narrative of the Life of Olaudah Equiano, or Gustavus Vassa, the African* (Leeds, England,1814), reprinted in Henry Louis Gates, Jr., ed., *The Classic Slave Narratives* (New York: Mentor, 1987), 25–26, 32–33.

pp. 21–22 William Waller Hening, ed., *The Statutes at Large, Being a Collection of the Laws of Virginia* (New York, R. & W. & G. Bartow, 1823), vol. 2:481–82.

pp. 22–25 Hening, *The Statutes at Large*, vol. 3:86–87.

pp. 25–26 Donald R. Lennon and Ida Brooks Kalman, eds., *The Wilmington Town Book 1743–1778* (Raleigh: North Carolina Division of Archives and History, 1973), 204–5.

p. 26 *Pennsylvania Gazette*, March 5, 1745.

pp. 26–27 *The Journal of Nicholas Cresswell, 1774–1777* (New York: Dial, 1924), 18–19.

pp. 28–29 William Moraley, *The Infortunate* (Newcastle, Del., 1743), reprinted in Susan E. Klepp and Billy G. Smith, eds., *The Infortunate: The Voyages and Adventures of William Moraley, an Indentured Servant* (University Park: Pennsylvania State University Press, 1992), 93–96.

pp. 30–32 Governor Robert Hunter to the Lords of Trade, June 23, 1712, in E. B. O'Callaghan ed., *Documents Relative to the Colonial History of the State of New York* (Albany, N.Y.: Weed, Parsons, 1854), vol. 5:341.

pp. 32–33 *Pennsylvania Gazette*, March 11, 1731. Reprinted in Billy G. Smith, ed., *Blacks Who Stole Themselves, Advertisements for Runaways in the Pennsylvania Gazette 1728–1790* (Philadelphia: University of Pennsylvania Press, 1992), 17.

p. 33 Smith, ed., *Blacks Who Stole Themselves*, 48.

pp. 36–38 Circular letter, Boston, 1773, New-York Historical Society. Facsimile in Sidney Kaplan and Emma Nogrady Kaplan, eds., *The Black Presence in the Era of the American Revolution*, (Amherst: University of Massachusetts Press, 1987), 14.

pp. 39–40 Phillis Wheatley, *Poems on Various Subjects, Religious and Moral* (London, 1773), 18, 73–75.

p. 41 Larry R. Gerlach, ed., *New Jersey in the American Revolution*, (Trenton: New Jersey Historical Commission, 1975), 150.

pp. 41–42 *Virginia Gazette*, November 16, 1775. Facsimile in Kaplan and Kaplan, eds., *The Black Presence*, 75.

pp. 42–43 Lord Dunmore, proclamation of November 1775. Facsimile in Kaplan and Kaplan, eds., *The Black Presence*, 74.

pp. 43–44 Peter Force, ed., *American Archives* (Washington, D.C., 1837–53), 6th ser., vol. 4:201–2.

p. 45 Whitfield J. Bell, Jr., ed., *The Declaration of Independence: Four 1776 Versions* (Philadelphia: American Philosophical Society, 1986).

pp. 46–47 Ruth Bogin, "'Liberty Further Extended': A 1776 Antislavery Manuscript by Lemuel Haynes," *William and Mary Quarterly*, 3d ser., vol. 40 (1983): 93–95. (By permission of the Houghton Library, Harvard University, bMS Am 1907, no. 608.)

p. 47 Joseph Plumb Martin, *Private Yankee Doodle*, George F. Scheer, ed. (Boston: Little Brown, 1962), 56.

pp. 48–52 *Methodist Magazine*, vol. 21 (1798):106–10.

pp. 52–54 John C. Dann, ed., *The Revolution Remembered* (Chicago: University of Chicago Press, 1980), 27–28.

pp. 55–56 Merrill Peterson, ed., *The Portable Thomas Jefferson* (New York: Penguin, 1975), 184–89.

pp. 56–60 Gary B. Nash, *Race and Revolution* (Madison, Wis.: Madison House, 1990), 177–81.

pp. 60–61 Afro-American Collection, New Haven Colony Historical Society.

p. 61 Robert Sutcliff, *Travels in Some Parts of North America, in the Years 1804, 1805, & 1806* (York, England, 1811), 50.

pp. 66–69 William Patten, *A Sermon, Delivered at the Request of the African Benevolent Society* (Newport, R.I., 1808), 13–15.

pp. 69–70 *Carolina Centinel* (Newbern, N.C.), January 15, 1820.

pp. 70–71 Henry Sipkins, *An Oration on the Abolition of the Slave Trade* (1809), reprinted in Dorothy Porter, ed., *Early Negro Writing, 1760–1857* (1971). Reprint (Baltimore: Black Classic Press, 1995), 372–73.

pp. 71–72 *Columbian Centinel* (Boston), July 18, 1821.

pp. 72–73 *Christian Repository* (Wilmington, Del.), September 6, 1821.

pp. 74–75 William Lloyd Garrison, *Thoughts on African Colonization; or, an Impartial Exhibition of the Doctrines, Principles and Purposes of the American Colonization Society. Together with Resolutions, Addresses and Remonstrances of the Free People of Color* (Boston: Garrison & Knapp, 1832), vol. 2:9–10.

pp. 76–77 David Walker, *David Walker's Appeal to the Coloured Citizens of the World* (New York: Hill & Wang, 1995), 69–71.

pp. 78–81 Marilyn Richardson, ed., *Maria W. Stewart, America's First Black Woman Political Writer* (Bloomington: Indiana University Press, 1987), 44–49.

pp. 82–83 *Proceedings of the Black State Conventions, 1830–65*, Philip S. Forer and George E. Walker, eds. (Philadelphia: Temple University Press, 1979), 38–39.

pp. 84–85 Herbert Aptheker, ed., *A Documentary History of the Negro People in the United States* (New York: Citadel, 1951), 137-38.

pp. 86–89 Frederick Douglass, "What to the Slave Is the Fourth of July?" in Douglass, *My Bondage and My Freedom* (New York, 1857), 441–46.

pp. 89–91 *New York Tribune*, July 19, 1854.

pp. 91–92 C. Peter Ripley, ed., *Witness for Freedom* (Chapel Hill: University of North Carolina Press, 1993), 70–71.

pp. 93–95 Martin R. Delany, *The Condition, Elevation, Emigration, and Destiny of the Colored People of the United States* (Philadelphia, 1852), 26–30.

pp. 108–10 Jack P. Greene, ed., *The Diary of Landon Carter* (Charlottesville: University Press of Virginia, 1965), 760–62.

pp. 111–14 H. W. Flourney, ed., *Calendar of Virginia State Papers* (Richmond, 1890), vol. 9:150–52, 164–65.

pp. 114–15 Rachel Blanding to Hannah Lewis, July 4, July 25, 1816, William Blanding Papers, South Caroliniana Library, University of South Carolina.

p. 116 Henry W. DeSaussure to Timothy Ford, July 9, 1816, Ford-Ravenel Papers, South Carolina Historical Society.

pp. 116–18 John Blassingame, ed., *Slave Testimony* (Baton Rouge: Louisiana State University Press, 1977), 66–68.

p. 119 Ulrich B. Phillips, ed., *Plantation and Frontier Documents, 1649–1863* (1910). Reprint (New York: Burt Franklin, 1968), vol. 1:320–21.

p. 120 Phillips, ed., *Plantation and Frontier Documents*, vol. 2: 45–46.

pp. 120–21 Gilbert Osofsky, ed., *Puttin' On Ole Massa: The Slave Narratives of Henry Bibb, William Wells Brown, and Solomon Northup* (New York: Harper & Row, 1969), 25–26.

p. 121 Osofsky, ed., *Puttin' On Ole Massa*, 22.

pp. 122–27 Frederick Douglass, *Narrative of the Life of Frederick Douglass, an American Slave* (Boston, 1846). Reprint (New York: Penguin, 1982), 78–79, 81–87.

pp. 128–32 Harriet A. Jacobs, *Incidents in the Life of a Slave Girl Written by Herself*, Jean Fagan Yellin, ed. (Cambridge: Harvard University Press, 1987), 27–28, 53–56.

pp. 133–135 William Still, *The Underground Railroad* (Philadephia: Porter & Coates, 1872), 81–84.

pp. 139–48 W. U. Hensel, *The Christiana Riot and the Treason Trials of 1851*, 2nd ed. (Lancaster, Pa.: New Era, 1911), 104–15.

pp. 148–49 *Christian Evangelist* (Oberlin, Ohio), Dececmber 21, 1859.

pp.149–50 William Cooper Nell, *Colored Patriots of the American Revolution* (Boston, 1855), 380–81.

pp. 150–51 Susie King Taylor, *A Black Woman's Civil War Memoirs*, Patricia W. Romero, ed., (New York: Markus Weiner, 1988), 31–32.

pp. 151-52 Herbert Aptheker, ed., *A Documentary History of the Negro People in the United States* (New York: Citadel, 1951), 464.

pp. 151–52 Aptheker, ed., *Documentary History*, 470.

pp. 154–55 Ira Berlin, et al., eds., *Free at Last* (New York: New Press, 1992), 61–62.

pp. 156–57 Don E. Fehrenbacher, ed., *Abraham Lincoln: A Documentary Portrait* (Stanford, Calif.: Stanford University Press, 1964), 195–96.

pp. 157–58 Berlin, ed., *Free at Last*, 99.

pp. 158–59 Brenda Stevenson, ed., *The Journals of Charlotte Forten Grimké* (New York: Oxford University Press, 1988), 428–32.

p. 159–60 *The War of the Rebellion: A Compilation of the Official Records of the Union and Confederate Armies* (Washington, D.C.: Government Printing Office, 1885), ser. 1, vol. 14:196, 198.

p. 160 Thomas Wentworth Higginson, *Army Life in a Black Regiment* (New York: Norton, 1984), 45–46.

pp. 161–62 Edwin S. Redkey, ed., *A Grand Army of Black Men: Letters from African American Soldiers in the Union Army* (New York: Cambridge University Press, 1992), 47–48.

pp. 162–63 Redkey, ed., *A Grand Army*, 166.

## Sidebar Text

pp. 17, 22 Bartlett Burleigh James and J. Franklin Jameson, eds., *Journal of Jasper Danckaerts* (New York: Scribner's, 1913), 65, 133.

p. 19 Hugh Jones, *History of the Present State of Virginia*, Richard L. Morton, ed. (Chapel Hill: University of North Carolina Press, 1956).

p. 25 David Brion Davis, *The Problem of Slavery in Western Culture* (Ithaca, N.Y.: Cornell University Press, 1966), 118.

p. 36 *New Jersey Gazette*, September 20, 1780. Reprinted in Larry R. Gerlach, ed., *New Jersey in the American Revolution* (Trenton: New Jersey Historical Commission, 1975), 437.

p. 38 William L. Saulser, ed., *Colonial Records of North Carolina* (Raleigh, N.C., 1890), vol. 10:138.

p. 39 Phillis Wheatley, *Poems on Various Subjects, Religious and Moral* (London, 1773), vii.

p. 41 Sylvia R. Frey, *Water from the Rock: Black Resistance in a Revolutionary Age* (Princeton, N.J.: Princeton University Press, 1991), 113–14.

p. 48 Sidney Kaplan and Emma Nogrady Kaplan, *The Black Presence in the Era of the American Revolution*, rev. ed. (Amherst: University of Massachusetts Press, 1987), 73.

p. 59 *Georgetown Weekly Ledger*, March 1791.

p. 66 Dorothy Sterling, ed., *We Are Your Sisters: Black Women in the Nineteenth Century* (New York: Norton, 1984), 114.

p. 68 Gary B. Nash, *Race and Revolution* (Madison, Wis.: Madison House, 1990), 196.

p. 71 Herbert Aptheker, ed., *A Documentary History of the Negro People in the United States* (New York: Citadel, 1951), 108.

p. 73 Jane H. Pease and William H. Pease, eds., *The Antislavery Argument* (Indianapolis: Bobbs-Merrill, 1965), 21.

p. 74 Merrill Peterson, ed., *Democracy, Liberty and Property: The State Constitutional Conventions of the 1820s* (Indianapolis: Bobbs-Merrill, 1966), 228.

p. 79 Dorothy Porter, ed., *Early Negro Writing, 1760–1837* (Boston: Beacon, 1971), 295.

p. 108 From "The Story of Mattie J. Jackson" (1869), 10. In *Six Women's Slave Narratives* (New York: Oxford University Press, 1988).

p. 111 John Mellor, ed., *Bullwhip Days: The Slaves Remember* (New York: Weidenfeld & Nicholson, 1988), 198.

p. 114 Mellor, ed., *Bullwhip Days*, 200.

p. 116 Lionel H. Kennedy and Thomas Parker, eds., *An Official Report of Sundry Negroes, Charged with an Attempt to Raise an Insurrection in the State of South Carolina* (Charleston, S.C., 1822). Reprint, *The Trial Record of Denmark Vesey* (Boston: Beacon, 1970), 11.

p. 117 Douglass, *Narrative*, 35.

p. 120 Paul F. Paskoff and Daniel J. Wilson, eds., *The Cause of the South: Selections from DeBow's Review* (Baton Rouge: Louisiana State University Press, 1982), 21.

p. 142 Charles Emery Stevens, *Anthony Burns: A History* (Boston: John P. Jewett and Co., 1856), 281.

p. 144 Martin R. Delany, *The Condition, Elevation, Emigration, and Destiny of the Colored People of the United States* (Philadelphia, 1852), 155.

p. 149 Paul Finkelman, ed., *His Soul Goes Marching On: Responses to John Brown and the Harpers Ferry Raid* (Charlottesville: University Press of Virginia, 1995), 64.

p. 150 John Mellor, ed., *Bullwhip Days: The Slaves Remember* (New York: Weidenfeld & Nicholson, 1988), *459*.

p. 152 C. Peter Ripley, ed., *Witness for Freedom* (Chapel Hill: University of North Carolina Press, 1993), 149–50.

p. 153 James M. McPherson, ed., *The Negro's Civil War* (New York: Ballantine, 1991), 38.

p. 155 Sterling, ed., *We Are Your Sisters*, 237–38.

p. 156 Edwin S. Redkey, ed., *A Grand Army of Black Men: Letters from African-American Soldiers in the Union Army, 1861–1865* (New York: Cambridge University Press, 1992), 172–73.

p. 157 Redkey, ed., *A Grand Army*, 208.

p. 159 Sterling, ed., *We Are Your Sisters*, 259.

# Picture Credits

Courtesy, American Antiquarian Society: 45, 50, 99 (top); Boston Athenaeum: 67, 84, 100 (top); Boston Public Library: 69; John Carter Brown Library at Brown University: 51; Chicago Historical Society: all on 103, 165 (right); The Connecticut Historical Society, Hartford, Connecticut: 53; Courtesy of Charleston Library Society, Charleston, S.C.: 32; Courtesy George Eastman House: both on 102 (bottom); Harvard Houghton Library: 115; The Library Company of Philadelphia: 9 (both), 18, 70, 151, 154 (all); Library of Congress: 11 (LC-USZ62-44265), 14, 21 (LC-USZ62-16876-201378), 40 left (LC-USZ62-40054), 46 (LC-USZ62-42043), 58 (LC-MS-27748), 68 (LC-229034), 72 (LC-USZ62-40688-228862), 77 (LC-USZ62-105530), 96 (LC-229955), 111 (LC-MS-55715), 117 (LC-USZ62-38902), 123 (neg. number 63896), 126, 134 (LC-USZ62-056053), 139 (LC-229036-713), 146 (LC-USZ62-75975), 148

(LC-USZ61-748), 158 (LC-B8171-2594), 163 (LC-USZ62-32314), 164 (left), 165 middle (LC-USZ62-38902); The Library of Virginia: 28, 109; Louisiana State University Special Collections: 155; The Maryland Historical Society, Baltimore, Maryland: 57, 118; Courtesy of the Massachusetts Historical Society: 37, 55, 62, 165 (left); All rights reserved, The Metropolitan Museum of Art: 81; Moores Memorial Library: 141; The Gilder Lehrman Collection at the Pierpoint Morgan Library: 34, 74, 87; © Museum of the City of New York: 121; New Bedford Whaling Museum: 100 (bottom); The Newport Historical Society: 16; Collection of the New-York Historical Society: 3 (neg. number 50479), 78 (neg. number 46594), 91, 99 bottom (neg. number 74735), 110 (neg. number 74736), 113 (neg. number 64317), 153; New York Public Library: 24, 75, 83, 98 (top and bottom), 101, 102 (top), 150; North Carolina Division

of Archives: 125; Nova Scotia Archives and Records Management: 49, 164 (right); Courtesy, Peabody & Essex Museum, Salem, Mass.: 19; Abby Aldrich Rockefeller Folk Art Museum, Williamsburg, Va.: 27, 119, 131; The Fine Arts Museums of San Francisco, Mildred Anna Williams Collection: 94; Courtesy of the Society for the Preservation of New England Antiquities: 2; Sophia Smith Collection, Smith College: cover, 71, 95, 149; South Carolina Department of Archives and History: 31; Historic Stagville, Division of Archives and History, N.C. Department of Cultural Resources: 129; Photography Collections, University of Maryland Baltimore County: 136, 159; Special Collections and Archives, W. E. B. Du Bois Library, University of Massachusetts Amherst: 40 (right); Virginia Historical Society: 43; Colonial Williamsburg Foundation: 106; Courtesy of Richard Bruce Winders: 104.

# Index

# Acknowledgments

Students at Bennington College and Yale University saw many of these documents first: their questions convinced me of the value of books like this one. My most important thanks go to two students in particular, who also served as my assistants. Lynn Murphy, my first sounding board for the project, did essential research, and typed in most of the documents. Her energy, enthusiasm, and intelligence helped get the project on its feet. Elizabeth Thorpe drafted document and chapter introductions for chapter 3, performed follow-up research, and with her sharp questions helped clarify my interpretations and my prose. It was a privilege to teach them and a pleasure to employ them. I would also like to thank Carol Karlsen, Sarah Deutsch, and Nancy Toff for making it happen and, with Lisa Barnett and especially Brigit Dermott, for their many suggestions, which much improved this book.

# About the Author

David Waldstreicher is an associate professor of history at the University of Notre Dame. He is the author of *In the Midst of Perpetual Fetes: The Making of American Nationalism, 1776–1820*, which won the Jamestown Prize of the Omohundro Institute of Early American History and Culture. Most recently he has edited an edition of Thomas Jefferson's *Notes on the State of Virginia and Related Documents*. In 2001 he was appointed a fellow at the center for Scholars and Writers at the New York Public Library, to work on his book *Runaway America: Benjamin Franklin, Slavery, and the American Revolution*.